D1570620

BAC SI

ME + My Dispensary

BAC SI

A GREEN BERET MEDIC'S WAR IN VIETNAM

Jerry Krizan & Robert Dumont

CASEMATE
Philadelphia & Oxford

Published in the United States of America and Great Britain in 2014 by
CASEMATE PUBLISHERS
908 Darby Road, Havertown, PA 19083
and
10 Hythe Bridge Street, Oxford, OX1 2EW

Copyright 2014 © Jerry Krizan and Robert Dumont

ISBN 978-1-61200-246-0
Digital Edition: ISBN 978-1-61200-247-7

Cataloging-in-publication data is available from the Library of Congress and
the British Library.

10 9 8 7 6 5 4 3 2 1

Printed and bound in the United States of America.

For a complete list of Casemate titles please contact:

CASEMATE PUBLISHERS (US)
Telephone (610) 853-9131, Fax (610) 853-9146
E-mail: casemate@casematepublishers.com

CASEMATE PUBLISHERS (UK)
Telephone (01865) 241249, Fax (01865) 794449
E-mail: casemate-uk@casematepublishing.co.uk

All photos property of the author, Jerry Krizan, unless otherwise noted.

Frontispiece: *Author Jerry Krizan in front of medical dispensary
after it was hit by mortar in August 1968.*

CONTENTS

ACKNOWLEDGMENTS

First, I want to salute all of the brave American men and women who served their country so honorably and so thanklessly in Vietnam. I am especially grateful to the US Army soldiers who in August 1968 fought their way north to Loc Ninh to prevent those of us at Special Forces Camp A-331 from being overrun by the NVA. I am also indebted to the members of the 11th Cav who saved my ass on more than one occasion.

I was inspired by my medic classmate and good friend Joseph Parnar to begin to write my own stories down. Joe helped me with many Vietnamese terms and spellings and along with Kyle Davidson, assisted in producing the maps.

Further inspiration and encouragement was received from Lieutenant Colonel Robert K. Brown, USAR (Ret.) editor/publisher of *Soldier of Fortune Magazine,* who published an earlier version of a chapter from this book in the February 2013 issue of *SOF.*

Thanks also go to my medic classmate Mike Erkel and to fellow medic and former teammate Tom Reisinger for refreshing my memory with facts and details from so long ago.

Enough appreciation cannot go to my collaborator Robert Dumont who has edited and revised my stories and corrected my grammar. Bob continued to work with me even when the prospects for success of this project seemed to be remote at best.

Finally, thank you Casemate Publishing for allowing me to relate my Vietnam experiences.

—Jerry Krizan, *Kalamazoo, Michigan*

NORTH
VIETNAM

Demarcation Line

Quang Tri

● Hue

*South
China
Sea*

Thua Thien

● Da Nang

LAOS

Quang Nam

THAILAND

I CTZ

Quang Tin

Quang Ngai

Kontum

**SOUTH
VIETNAM**

Binh Dinh

Pleiku

*Tonle
Sap*

CAMBODIA

Phu Bon

Darlac

Phu Yen

Khanh
Hoa

II CTZ

Quang Duc

Tuyen Duc
Da Lat ●

● Cam Ranh

Phuoc
Long

Ninh
Thuan

Binh
Long

Lam Dong

Tay Ninh

III CTZ

Binh
Duong

Long
Khanh

Binh
Tuy

Binh Thuan

Hua
Nghia

Bien
Hoa

Kien Tuong

Kien Phong

Long
An

★ Saigon

Gia
Dinh

Phuoc
Tuy

Chau
Doc

Dinh Tuong

Go
Cong

● Vung Tau

An
Giang

Sa
Dec

Kien Giang

Vinh
Long

Kien Hoa

Phong
Dinh

*Gulf
of
Thailand*

IV CTZ

Chuong
Thien

Vinh Binh

Ba Xuyen

Bac Lieu

An Xuyen

South Vietnam
1966–1967

—— CORPS TACTICAL ZONE BOUNDARY

——·—— ADMINISTRATIVE BOUNDARY

● AUTONOMOUS MUNICIPALITY

0   150 miles

0   150 km

Mekong R.

FOREWORD

J ERRY KRIZAN AND I first met when we both volunteered to undertake US Army Special Forces medical training in February of 1967. The medics training course was the longest of the Special Forces disciplines and lasted for 37 weeks.

Our training started with all volunteers for Special Forces, including those pursuing an MOS (Military Occupational Specialty) in Communications, Weapons, Engineering, Organization and Intelligence, or Medical, undergoing four weeks of field exercises and general instruction. This covered such areas as map reading, land navigation, patrolling, setting up ambushes, reconnaissance, and other military skills. It was after these four weeks of training that we were issued our Green Berets. We were not permitted to mount our Special Forces crests on a group flash background on the beret however, as that distinction was reserved only for those who had completed training and were assigned to a Special Forces Group. The Special Forces crest with no flash background insured that everyone knew we were still trainees assigned to Training Group.

Medics training began with an eight-week course in anatomy and medical terminology conducted at Fort Bragg and taught by medical non-commissioned officers (NCO's) from Special Forces. As would be the method of instruction for all of our remaining medical course work, the material covered each week was tested with an exam every Friday. Anyone who could not maintain a 70% grade average was cut from medics training.

After anatomy and medical terminology, we went to Brooke Army Hospital at Fort Sam Houston in San Antonio, Texas for the ten-week Special Forces medical training conducted by Army doctors. This course covered the essentials of medical diagnosis and treatment. After completing it we were fully qualified Army medics.

The next phase of training was seven weeks of "On the Job Training" [OJT] at one of the Army's medical centers located throughout the United States. Jerry and I were both assigned to the Ireland Army Hospital at Fort Knox, Kentucky along with six of our classmates.

After OJT, our entire medics class was reunited at Fort Bragg for six weeks of instruction on the diagnosis and treatment of tropical diseases. This was followed by "Dog Lab," a course in surgery using dogs as patients. Our final exam was to appear before a review board made up of six Army doctors and one NCO who could ask questions about anything covered at any stage of our training.

Another three weeks of classes on Special Forces operations and procedures culminated with a week of field maneuvers at Camp McCall that ended with a 30-mile hike to be completed in 24 hours. After graduation, we were each assigned to one of the Special Forces Groups.

I am especially glad that Jerry is putting his experiences in Vietnam together for this book. I did not serve on an A-Team in Vietnam, the basic operating unit of Special Forces during the Vietnam War, and have often wondered what being at an A-Team camp was like. Jerry's accounts relate not only the duties of the medics at the A-Team camps but also the high volume of combat to which they were exposed.

His book is a valuable addition to the history of Army Special Forces and the A-Team camps in Vietnam.

—Joe Parnar, Gardner, Massachusetts; author of *SOG MEDIC: Stories From Vietnam and Over the Fence*, Paladin Press 2007.

INTRODUCTION — BACKGROUND

M Y NAME IS Jerry Krizan. From May 1968 to May 1969 I served in the United States Army with Special Forces Detachment A-331 (A-Team), at Camp Loc Ninh, Binh Long Province, Republic of Vietnam. I was a Special Forces Medic, MOS (Military Occupational Specialty) 91B4S, having received my Special Forces and medics training at Fort Bragg, North Carolina.

I had additional clinical training at Fort Sam Houston in San Antonio, Texas and served an internship at the Ireland Army Hospital at Fort Knox, Kentucky. In writing this I am not attempting to give away any military secrets but only to relate some of my experiences as a Green Beret soldier and medic while serving my country during the war in Vietnam.

For purposes of military operations, South Vietnam was divided into four Corps Tactical Zones or Military Regions. The four CTZs were separated by imaginary lines dividing the country from the north to the south. They were designated as I-Corps (pronounced "Eye-Corps") in the north and adjacent to the DMZ (De-Militarized Zone); II-Corps extended from the Central Highlands to the lowlands near the South China Sea; III-Corps included Saigon, the nation's capital, and 11 surrounding provinces; and IV-Corps covered the Mekong River Delta.

Because it was impossible to seal South Vietnam's more than 900 miles of land boundaries, one of the measures that MACV (Military Assistance Command Vietnam) undertook to secure the countryside was to expand a program that began initially under the sponsorship of the CIA. Isolated outposts or camps in the border regions were established and manned by members of the Civilian Irregular Defense Group. The CIDG was comprised mostly of ethnic minorities living in these regions with members of the US Army Special Forces acting as "advisors."

All SF activities in Vietnam operated under the command of the 5th Special Forces Group (Airborne), headquartered in Nha Trang in II-Corps. Each Corp Tactical Zone had a Special Forces C-Team, consisting of approximately 70 Special Forces personnel under the command of a lieutenant colonel. The C-Team had administrative and logistical control over a number of B-Teams. Located throughout the Corps area, though typically in a provincial capital, B-Teams consisted of approximately 30 Special Forces personnel. The B-Teams in turn oversaw the activities of four to five A-Teams. The C- and B-Teams were not combat units *per se* but did have some indigenous troops posted to provide protection.

In the III-Corps area where I was stationed, the C-Team headquarters was in Bien Hoa, 30 miles northeast of Saigon. Our B-Team was at An Loc on Highway 13, approximately 65 miles directly north of Saigon and 13 miles directly south of Loc Ninh.

The A-Team at Camp Loc Ninh was designated A-331. The A stood for A-Team, the first 3 stood for III Corps, the second 3 stood for our B-Team (B-33), and the 1 stood for the individual A-Team number reporting to the B-Team. The individual A-Teams were responsible for conducting combat operations and field intelligence gathering of enemy troop movements in their individual area of operations (AO's) within the B-Team's larger AO.

The typical A-Team in Vietnam was made up of 12 men—10 enlisted men and two officers. The enlisted men consisted of a team sergeant, an intelligence specialist, two communications specialists, two medical specialists, two demolitions specialists, a heavy weapons and a light weapons specialist. The junior enlisted men in each specialty could range in rank from Sp4 to staff sergeant. The seniors could range from staff sergeant to sergeant first class, with the team sergeant usually being a master sergeant. The officers were a team commander, usually a captain or first lieutenant; and an executive officer, usually a first or second lieutenant. When I arrived at A-331 I had the rank of Sergeant E-5 and was the junior medical specialist.

Camp Loc Ninh was located in the middle of an old French rubber plantation a half-mile southwest of the village of Loc Ninh. The rubber plantation extended three to four miles in each direction and beyond it was the jungle. The camp was in a part of Binh Long Province that jutted out slightly to the north and west, making the border with Cambodia approximately 10 miles distant. The part of Cambodia that lay directly south and west of us and extended into Vietnam was called the "Fish Hook" and was believed to be the location of the North Vietnamese Army's mobile operational headquarters for South Vietnam during the war. Loc Ninh was thus on a main infiltration route for the NVA, which they would use when moving out from their sanctuaries in Cambodia to mount attacks on An Loc, Bien Hoa, and Saigon.

The primary mission of a United States Army Special Forces A-Team, whether in Vietnam or in a major world war, was to train, equip, and arm a battalion-size group of approximately 500 indigenous personnel and to mold them into a combat-ready force. The team members were all experts in their individual Army specialties and were also excellent teachers and instructors. The team's goal was to get the indigenous troops trained to a high skill level and be able to function as an independent fighting unit.

In a major war, the A-Team, along with the trained indigenous forces, were to function as guerrillas until such time as the tide of battle changed and they would then function as a regular army unit. Special Forces expertise in irregular warfare is one of the reasons that A-Teams operated in Vietnam. Who better to fight the Viet Cong guerrillas than soldiers trained in guerrilla warfare?

My specialty, Special Forces Medic, is somewhat of a misnomer. A Special Forces Medic was actually classified as a "Special Forces Aidman." Per general rules of warfare, Army medics or Navy corpsmen were not allowed to carry offensive weapons, though some were permitted to have a .45 caliber pistol for personal protection. Medics or corpsmen wore a Red Cross insignia and were able to participate in combat operations, but only to assist and treat the wounded.

A Special Forces Aidman, of which I was one, did not wear a Red Cross insignia and could carry offensive weapons and was fully involved in combat operations along with the other members on the A-Team. The Medic

(Aidman) performed various medical duties in camp, but if the camp was under attack or an operation in the field resulted in contact with the enemy, the Aidman played an active combat role. Then once the fighting was over, his medical duties kicked in.

The official role of US Special Forces (Green Berets) in Vietnam was in an advisory capacity to the Vietnamese Special Forces, the *Luc Luong Dac Biet* (LLDB). At Loc Ninh we had a detachment of Vietnamese Special Forces and each of our specialties (medical, communications, etc.) had an LLDB counterpart. My own LLDB counterpart was a large Vietnamese fellow of Chinese extraction named *Bac Si* Cong. *Bac Si* means doctor or medic in the Vietnamese language and it wasn't long after I arrived that I too was being referred to by that appellation.

Each operation in the field consisted of two Americans, an LLDB, and a multi-company or platoon made up of members of the Civilian Irregular Defense Group who we Americans called CIDs, (pronounced "sids"). The reason why two Americans always went into the field was that we could not count on the CIDs or our LLDB counterparts for help if one of us got hit. We basically were there to cover each other's back. Officially, our role on an operation was advisory, although we also had to coordinate and call in American artillery and air support if we were in contact with the enemy. Unofficially, once we were in contact, it was the Americans who were in charge as the LLDBs (nicknamed Lousy Little Dirty Bugouts) were often nowhere to be found once the shooting started.

The regular troops in the camp, the CIDs, were divided into seven operational units. We had five companies of 125 CIDs and two recon platoons of 35 CIDs each. Each company had its own CIDG commander and platoon leaders. I eventually knew who the company commanders were but was never able to figure out who all the platoon leaders were. The two recon platoons were each a mix of Vietnamese, Montagnards, and Cambodians—allegedly the cream of the crop.

The companies were a lot more segregated, with two companies consisting exclusively of Vietnamese and Montagnard CIDs, two companies consisting of Komerceri Cambodians, and one company consisting exclusively of Khrum Kampuchea Khmer (KKK).

Most of the members of the two companies of mixed Vietnamese and Montagnard personnel had been rounded up years before in the Saigon area and sent to Loc Ninh to serve their country. There were also some local Vietnamese and Montagnards who had joined us to avoid getting drafted by the ARVN (Army of the Republic of Vietnam) or being captured and forced to join the local VC (Viet Cong).

The Komerceri Cambodians had fled from a civil war in that country in the 1950's and sought refuge in Vietnam. The border between Vietnam and Cambodia was well defined on the map but meant little to the people living near it. It was a lawless and unexplored area. The Komerceri were the best fighters, led by hardcore commanders. Their mission was to survive as a fighting force and to eventually re-take Cambodia. The leader of the two Komerceri companies was essentially a warlord who was for now on our side.

The KKK were Cambodian Montagnards who had also fled during the Cambodian civil war. They were border bandits whose loyalties went to whoever paid them the most money. Of the total number of CIDs in camp, we figured that 5% of them were VC sympathizers, but with the KKK it might have been 20% or more. We were always careful around them when we were in contact with the enemy; we did not trust them and did not want to be taken out by one of our own troops.

US Army Special Forces in Vietnam ran other operations that were outside the A-Team chain of command. These operations varied from special strike forces in each of the four Corp Tactical Zones to classified reconnaissance missions "across the fence" into Laos and Cambodia along the Ho Chi Minh Trail. Although I am familiar with these operations, I am only relating my own personal experiences as a Special Forces medic on an A-Team in Vietnam.

Aerial view of Camp Loc Ninh A-331 in September 1967. Courtesy US Air Force

CHAPTER 1

THE JOURNEY TO SPECIAL FORCES

W HEN I WAS A young boy growing up my friends and I would play army or cowboys and Indians but I never had any great desire or ambition to actually join the military. When I was in high school, during the Cold War between the United States and Russia, it was the dawn of the "space age" and the era of the "space race" between the two countries. I was properly brainwashed to believe that I had to go to college and become an engineer. I was the first person in my family to go to college and neither my parents nor I had a clue what that entailed.

Upon graduation from high school I enrolled at Muskegon Junior College and majored in Engineering. I also had to get a job in a grocery store to pay for my education. After a year and a half I realized that I had no real enthusiasm for becoming an engineer and switched my major to Accounting. I did better in Accounting and completed the coursework in December 1964. I then applied for admission to Western Michigan University and was accepted for the fall semester of 1965. Between the completion of the courses at MJC and the start of school at Western in September, I was out of school for several months and received my first real exposure to the Army.

Like every male in America I had registered with the Selective Service System (Draft Board) when I turned 18. I lost my student deferment because I was not currently enrolled in college and was ordered to report to the Muskegon National Guard Armory where I would be bussed to Fort Wayne in Detroit to receive a "Pre-Induction Physical." This meant that the Muskegon Draft Board had its sights set on me. If I passed the physical,

I could expect to receive "greetings" (draft notice) in the mail, unless I got back in college and renewed my student deferment.

The pre-induction physical involved standing around in your underwear all day with a couple hundred other young men from all walks of life from all over Michigan. There was a written test where I sat next to a guy who was actually trying to join the Army but he could not read and write. He could barely print his own name. I was blown away. I had never met anyone who could not read and write. I tried to help him with the test but I don't think he passed. Later, we all stood in a line as a doctor came along and touched everyone's chest with a stethoscope for maybe five seconds to check our lungs and heart. If you were breathing and warm to the touch, you were judged to be fit. When the physical was over I boarded a bus, along with some other guys, that took us back to Muskegon.

I started classes at Western Michigan in the fall and received my student draft deferment status from the Draft Board. I was safe from the Army for the time being and did not give it another thought. I noticed that quite a few guys in my dorm at Western were in college just to avoid the draft. They were not real college material and I viewed them as a bunch of crazy guys having a good time. I turned down an offer to join a rock band that was being formed in the dorms because I wanted to concentrate on my studies and because I did not have $500.00 for the amp I would need.

My problems began in February when I turned 21 (legal drinking age) and my grades went downhill from there. I thought I had my grade point averages all figured out well enough to stay in school but an unexpected low grade from a Business Law class during the winter semester did me in. Western Michigan University asked me to take a semester off, to reflect, I guess. I could re-enroll for the winter semester the next year.

Of course, that meant I would lose my student deferment for the summer and fall semesters because at that time draft boards did not consider the fact that you were planning to return to college. As far as they were concerned I was no longer a student because I was not currently enrolled in school. So I was screwed!

I returned home to Muskegon and got a job in a piston ring factory and started to ponder my options. I was a college guy and I knew I was going to be drafted. If you were drafted into the Army it was a two-year obligation. If you joined the Army, it was a three-year obligation. But I also figured that since I was a college guy, I should probably go to OCS (Officers Candidate School). One could go to OCS if you were qualified, once you went through Basic Training and Advanced Training. OCS took about six months and then you had to re-enlist for two years upon completion.

So either option—getting drafted and going to OCS or enlisting and going to OCS—meant I was looking at three years of military service.

At the end of June I received a draft notice in the mail. "Greetings, your friends and neighbors have selected you . . . blah, blah, blah." I was to report for induction into the Army at the end of July. I had also, a couple weeks earlier, gotten laid off from the piston ring company and had no money. I thought it would improve my chances for OCS if I enlisted immediately instead of being drafted. And that's what I did. I signed the papers and was bused down to Fort Wayne for another physical and was inducted into the US Army on July 7, 1966.

From there it was off to Fort Leonard Wood for eight weeks of Basic Training. We learned to salute, march, stand at attention, and fire an M-14 rifle in the hot Missouri sun. Toward the end of Basic, the drill sergeants passed out an application to attend a two-week Leadership Preparation Class course prior to AIT (Advanced Infantry Training). Completing the course would enable you to be an acting barracks NCO (Non-Commissioned Officer) during AIT. It sounded like something I would like to do.

I filled out the form and turned it in to the sergeant who was seated at a picnic table. Afterwards, as I was sitting on the ground resting against a tree, I saw a piece of paper blowing in the breeze. I went over and picked it up. It was my application for the leadership course. I took it to the drill sergeant and he once again put it on the pile of applications. If I had not seen my application being blown away I would not have gone to the leadership course.

Upon graduation from Basic, I was given a short leave home, and then it was on to Fort Ord, California.

Fort Ord at that time was the Pre-Officer Candidate School AIT. Guys who had enlisted normally got to choose a specialty and would go on to Specialist Training Schools after Basic Training. They would learn cooking, truck driving, mechanics, etc., whatever skills were necessary for them to perform their duties in the Army. A regular draftee after Basic would typically be assigned to the Infantry and go to AIT at a place like Fort Polk,

Louisiana. After Fort Polk they could expect to receive a 30-day leave and then be off to Vietnam to serve for a year as a rifleman in an infantry company. Those of us at Fort Ord were generally already signed up to go to OCS and upon graduation from AIT would be shipped off to an OCS school.

The two-week Leadership Preparation Class went well and upon graduation I was assigned to a training platoon. During the first week of AIT, I was the second-in-command of the 2nd Platoon and was promoted to be acting platoon sergeant the following week. About a third of the guys in the platoon had college degrees and the rest of us, with one exception, had completed two or three years of college. Second Platoon was the best in the company—we won the "Best Platoon Award" seven weeks out of the eight week training period.

After the first couple of weeks of AIT, I was regularly called in to see the company commander and the master sergeant. They praised me for the excellent job that I was doing and told me what a great officer I was going to make. They even said that the one week my platoon did not receive the Best Platoon Award (though we deserved it), was just so the other platoons would not give up.

But I didn't exactly do everything the conventional Army way.

In the leadership course we were taught to vary each man's responsibility

Joe Parner, right, and author Jerry Krizan, left, on leave in summer of 1967.

in cleaning the barracks so that they would not get bored. My thinking was, "Come on now, we are all college guys and whether you clean a toilet or mop the floor it doesn't matter, it's still menial and uninteresting work."

So I assigned each person his cleaning task for the whole eight weeks. One guy was assigned to clean two toilets, another guy the other two toilets; a couple of guys were to clean the shower, a couple of guys were to mop, and a couple of guys were to buff the floor. Everyone had a specific responsibility and once they were done I told them to "disappear until morning formation." Even in the breakfast chow line we lined up according to our assignment in the order that it had to be completed so that we would not be tripping over each other. For example, the toilet and sink cleaners ate before the guys that mopped the floor. That way the toilets and sinks would be done and they would be out of the latrine by the time the mop guys arrived and did their job. Maybe it was not the Army way but it worked and was efficient.

I had only a few doubts regarding my decision to join the Army and go to OCS when I was in Basic Training and started to see how things worked. But now in AIT, the idea of being an officer and having to go fight a war in Vietnam was becoming very unsettling. The war in Vietnam had not even entered into my decision when I enlisted, but it was heavily emphasized in Advanced Infantry Training. I began to realize that there really was a war going on in Asia and we were being trained to fight in it. The possibility that I could be killed or seriously wounded started to sink in.

I did not have a warm and fuzzy feeling about being a private in the infantry, if I were to ditch OCS. But the prospect of completing OCS and becoming a 2nd Lieutenant did not set my mind at rest either. I began to think that if I did have to go and fight in Vietnam, I should be as highly trained as possible, which would increase my chances of survival.

One afternoon when no training was scheduled I was assigned the duty of marching 30 of my fellow trainees to the supply facility to get new boots and uniforms. I marched them over, waited for them to be issued their new gear, and then marched them back to the company area. When I returned, I found out that a Special Forces sergeant had spoken to the rest of the assembled company while I was gone. He had talked about Special

Forces and invited anyone who was interested in joining to accompany him back to his office where he would give them a written test to see if they qualified. I asked the company commander and the company master sergeant what Special Forces was like and they told me that I would not be interested since I was going on to OCS. But the idea of Special Forces got my curiosity going because I knew they were highly skilled.

That evening I wandered over to the SF sergeant's office and talked to him. He provided me with a short run-down on the training and gave me the written test. I passed it with flying colors. The more I thought about it, the more it seemed that Special Forces would give me a better chance of survival in Vietnam than the OCS option.

I signed up for Special Forces immediately but things did not go down so good when the paperwork came over to my training company. The CO and company sergeant were all over my case for passing up OCS. They were not at all happy with me and tried to convince me that I was excellent officer material. But I had made up my mind.

Upon graduation from AIT my Special Forces training started. First up was three weeks of Airborne Jump School at Fort Benning, Georgia where I earned my jump wings. After jump school I was off to Fort Bragg, North Carolina. At Fort Bragg, all Special Forces recruits were given extensive written tests, and based on my test scores I was assigned to Medical, which was not my first choice. I wanted to be a demolition man and blow stuff up but I was not given that option.

But first I had one more hurdle to pass. I wore glasses. Apparently on the Army vision test, if you could read the top "E", and the "A" and "E" in the second line of the eye chart without glasses, you were deemed to be "Combat Qualified." But if you could not read them without glasses you were deemed to be "Non-Combat Qualified." I could always read the top two lines on an eye chart without my glasses, but somehow on the eye exam at jump school at Fort Benning my eye test indicated that I could not. And in order to be in Special Forces you needed to be combat qualified. When I was still processing-in at the Special Forces Training Group, a sergeant called me into his office:

He asked me, "Private Krizan do you want to be a Green Beret?"

I responded, "Yes sergeant I do."

He told me, "Well private, we have a problem. You flunked your eye test in jump school and you are therefore not combat qualified and we can't accept you into Special Forces. But I know private, in your file you passed all the other eye tests and would be qualified if this one test wasn't there. How bad do you want to be in Special Forces, private?"

"I want to join sergeant."

The sergeant then said, "Private Krizan, I'm going down the hall to get a cup of coffee. When I get back I'm going to review your vision tests. If they are okay you can start training. But if when I get back, you have an eye test in your folder that says you flunked, you're out of here."

The sergeant stared at me, was almost glaring, as he got up from his desk. He walked out the door and went down the hall. As soon as he left the room, I reached across the desk and grabbed my records folder. All the papers in it were attached by only two fasteners at the top. I found the eye test that I had flunked in jump school and ripped it out of the folder. I wadded it up and put it in the waste paper basket next to the desk. I then put the records folder back on the other side of the desk and sat back down in the chair to await the sergeant.

In about five minutes the sergeant returned and without a word sat down and opened up the folder. He briefly looked at the eye tests that remained in the folder. He looked up at me and said, "Welcome to Special Forces Private Krizan."

He dismissed me and I was approved to start training.

———————

Special Forces training lasted 41 weeks for the medical specialist course sequence. It began with a Special Forces Basic course and a medical course at Fort Bragg, followed by an additional medical course at Fort Sam Houston in San Antonio, Texas. OJT (On the Job Training) was at Fort Knox, Kentucky and then it was back to Fort Bragg for advanced medical training and a Tactics and Techniques course. On December 12, 1967 I graduated and was officially a Special Forces (Green Beret) Medic. I was assigned to the 7th Special Forces Group at Fort Bragg.

My three-year enlistment would be up in July 1969 and I had another great idea. If I volunteered to go to Vietnam for one year I could get an early out of the Army. The policy was that if you spent a year in Vietnam and returned to the States before your enlistment date was up, the Army would discharge you rather than sending you someplace for only two or three months.

I considered all of this and put in the paperwork and volunteered for service in Vietnam. I also realized that I was a highly trained soldier and that if I ever wanted to be in a war it was going to be now in Vietnam. I figured it would be the only war that I would experience in my lifetime and wanted to know if I had what it took—the courage to fight and to be brave. I didn't know if I did and I wanted to find out. I was not married and did not even have a girlfriend but I thought that if I ever did get married and have children, and if one day one of my children asked me "What did you do during the war daddy?" I wanted to give them an answer that they could be proud of.

I received my orders to go to Vietnam and was given a 30-day leave before I had to report to Fort Lewis, Washington. I headed back to Michigan and spent most of my time with my cousin Jeff, who was likewise on 30 day's leave after having spent a year in Vietnam with the Marine Corps. Jeff had served at the airstrip at Chu Lai. He was a Marine aircraft electrician and ordnance man for a squadron of F-4B Phantoms. He also flew as a helicopter door gunner with the Army. We hung out and went bowling a lot because we were bored. We didn't really discuss the war, except for one day while we were driving around and a loud siren went off. Jeff was behind the wheel and immediately stopped the car and ducked down.

I asked him, "Is this how I am going to be after Vietnam?"

"Yes," was his reply.

———

My Fort Lewis adventure began with a flight to the Seattle airport on standby, followed by a shared ride with a couple of other GI's from the airport to Fort Lewis in a cab that probably charged us about 10 times the regular fare. No doubt the Seattle cab drivers made good money fleecing the GI's.

At Fort Lewis, everyone who was being deployed to Vietnam, from 18-year old privates up to the rank of captain, was thrown together in the same barracks while awaiting processing. As I already had my orders to go to Vietnam and all my shots and records were up to date, it wasn't even an overnight for me. In a matter of hours I had been "processed" and was out of there.

I don't remember anyone talking about Vietnam. We were pushed from one station to another and then out the door. No gallows humor or anything. Just as well. We were too young and too stupid to know what really lay ahead.

I then got on a bus that took me and a bunch of other GI's to the airfield where we boarded a commercial aircraft that was to first fly us to Japan for refueling and a crew change. While at the barracks I had met up with a medics training classmate of mine, Tom Roe, and we sat together in the front row of the plane by the door along with another SF guy we knew. The front row seats had plenty of leg room and you could move around a lot better. The stewardess's jump seats for landing and takeoff were right in front of us. On the flight from Japan to Vietnam was a stewardess who we called "Twiggy." She was very thin and reminded everyone of the famous British model. Tom grew antsy and was always up helping the stewardesses in the galley most of the time. It gave him something to do.

He and I talked to Twiggy the whole flight until we landed at Tan Son Nhut Airbase outside of Saigon. As Tom and I were going out the door of the plane and down the stair ramp, we turned and said, "Good-bye Twiggy, see you in a year."

We saw that Twiggy was crying. With tears in her eyes, she said good-bye to us — a couple of young Green Berets going off to fight a war with the odds stacked against them that they would return home in one piece.

Author Jerry Krizan with parachute, ready to jump, 1967.
Courtesy Joseph Parnar

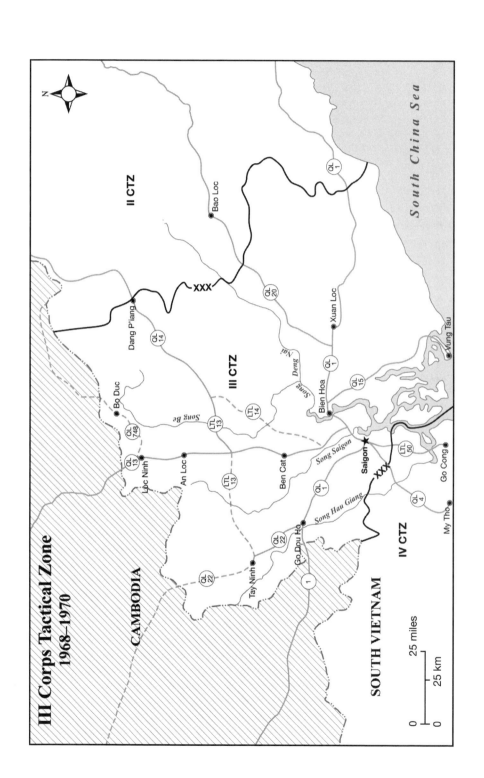

III Corps Tactical Zone
1968–1970

CAMBODIA

SOUTH VIETNAM

South China Sea

II CTZ

III CTZ

IV CTZ

Bao Loc

Dang P'iang

Bo Duc

Loc Ninh

An Loc

Tay Ninh

Go Dou Ho

Ben Cat

Saigon ★

Bien Hoa

Xuan Loc

Vung Tau

Go Cong

My Tho

Song Be

Song Dong Nai

Song Saigon

Song Hau Giang

QL 748

QL 13

QL 14

LTL 14

LTL 13

LTL 13

QL 22

QL 22

QL 1

QL 20

QL 1

QL 1

QL 15

LTL 50

QL 4

1

0   25 miles

0   25 km

CHAPTER 2

ARRIVAL AT LOC NINH

THE FIRST STOP IN Vietnam for Tom and me was the 5th Special Forces Group Headquarters in Nha Trang. We attended a 5th Group Vietnam orientation class for approximately a week that all new in-country SF personnel were required to attend. During that week we met up with Mike Erkel, a medic classmate of ours who was also newly arrived in Vietnam. In the final phase of the class the three of us were part of a group that was taken out to the hills north of Nha Trang, where we were to practice setting up a night ambush. This took place in a so-called safe area, and prior training exercises of this type had been uneventful. We were divided into three squads. Tom's was positioned at one ambush site and Mike's was set up at another. Mine was assigned to guard the headquarters and communications element of the ambush in an old abandoned French mansion.

In the middle of the night a reinforced VC squad walked into the ambush site where Tom was. Heavy gunfire broke out for a couple of minutes with the SF soldiers shooting from their concealed positions and the VC firing back. We had by chance ambushed the local VC payroll master and killed some of the VC squad members. Unfortunately, a young Special Forces lieutenant was hit by the VC return fire and also killed. He was the first casualty ever on the training course for the 5th Special Forces Group. Even though I did not fire my weapon during the encounter, some of my buddies did and the war became real.

We were given our assignments at Nha Trang when the orientation class was over. There were three open medic slots on A-Teams—one in I Corps, one in II Corps, and one in III Corps—and three medics to assign, Tom, Mike, and myself. Tom wanted to go to I Corps because his older brother was deployed there in an airborne unit. Mike really wanted to go to II Corps to work with the Montagnards. By default, and because I did not care where I went, I took the assignment in III Corps at an A-Team camp at Loc Ninh which I had never heard of before.

We said our goodbyes and good lucks then I was off to Bien Hoa where the C-Team for the III Corps area was headquartered. I received an orientation at the C-Team hospital and met the support staff there. The C-Team hospital was where all of the severely wounded Civilian Irregular Defense Group (CIDs) in the III Corps area was sent for surgery and recovery. Then it was off in the morning by helicopter to the B-Team at An Loc, and later in the afternoon, from An Loc by helicopter to where would be my new home for almost a year, the A-Team 331 at Loc Ninh.

I was a raw rookie in a combat zone in a foreign land. Though I was one of the most highly trained soldiers in the world, nothing in my medical, infantry, or tactical training in the regular Army or in Special Forces had prepared me mentally for the reality of being on an A-Team in Vietnam.

At Loc Ninh I was immediately issued an M-16 rifle and turned in the

Inner compound of Camp Loc Ninh; mortar pit is in the foreground and jeeps are in front of team quarters.

M-1 Carbine that I was issued at Nha Trang. I was assigned a bunk, met my teammates, and was given a general situation report for the Loc Ninh area of operation (AO). I sat in on a couple of morning sick calls for the troops and began to familiarize myself with the layout of the camp and to learn the camp and team rules, regulations, and SOP's (Standard Operating Procedures).

I got my first combat assignment. If we came under attack, the senior medic was supposed to be at the medical bunker, but I, as the junior medic, was assigned to the mortar pit located in the middle of the camp's inner compound. The senior medic was thus in a secure bunker safe from enemy small arms, rocket, or mortar fire while I was in an exposed combat position. My job was to inflict deadly mortar fire on the enemy.

This was just the way it worked on an A-Team—the senior commo man was in a secure communications bunker while the junior commo man was assigned a combat situation in the camp. A junior in rank could be assigned to a mortar pit, like me, or to a machine gun bunker, or to a section of the berm trench that surrounded the camp and was the main defensive position for the CIDs. I was assigned to the mortar pit solely because that is where the team needed an extra body.

The pit contained a 4.2-inch mortar and two 81mm mortars. The truth is I had never before even touched a real live mortar much less ever fired one. In my AIT Company at Fort Ord, 1st Platoon was the heavy weapons unit trained in the use of mortars but I had no idea what they did. So I was now receiving On the Job Training.

I had taken physics in high school and college and was pretty good in math, but even after my OJT I did not feel very confident about firing a mortar and being able to hit something with it. Fortunately, SFC Harvey Pipes, the senior weapons man, was the one computing the direction, range, elevation, and number of charges to put on the mortar round in order to strike a designated target.

Initially, I was the gopher on the fire mission. My main job was to go to the small ammo bunker in the pit and get out more mortar rounds then put the charges on the end of them. The number of charges put on the mortar round was calculated based on the distance to the target. The further away the target, the more charges were needed in order to reach it. Once they had the proper charges, I would bring the rounds to the mortar and either Harv or I would drop them down the tube and they would fire.

For defensive purposes, mortars were pre-aimed and the mortar rounds pre-charged to strike locations around the perimeter of the camp. All you had to do is drop a round down the tube and it would land in the predetermined area. You might then crank the mortar a couple of clicks to the right or the left to change the direction of the fire slightly and drop in another round. By dropping (firing) a round and moving the direction of the mortar fire over just a little, dropping another round, cranking a couple more clicks, and repeating this as fast as possible you would put a deadly ring of exploding mortar fire around a section of the perimeter. And once our teammates got to their defensive positions in the berm they could call in to the pit and direct the mortar fire on the enemy as well.

I got where I could manage all of this at my assigned post if called upon. Other mortars were pre-set to fire flares to illuminate the area near the camp in case of an attack and I got that down pat also. I felt pretty good. I had learned a new trade.

The third night I was in camp, the VC hit the village of Loc Ninh, attacking an RFPF (Regional Forces Popular Forces) guardhouse. The RFPF, called Ruff-Puffs by the Americans, were like a local militia. During the day they would strut and patrol all around the village but after dark they would usually retreat to their compound, which was a short distance up the road from us. So it was unusual that they actually had someone in the village in the guardhouse.

The VC hit the little outpost with AK-47 gunfire, RPG B-40 rockets, and 61mm mortar fire. The attack lasted approximately 10 minutes and we could hear it loud and clear from our camp a half-mile away.

I was in the team room when Top (the team sergeant) said to me, "*Bac Si*, they've got some civilian casualties from the village and they are bringing them into the dispensary. It's time for you to go earn your pay."

I high-tailed it down to the dispensary to do what I was trained to do, to treat the wounded. I arrived at the same time as an SFC (sergeant first class) nicknamed Doc', who was the acting senior medic onsite. The CID medics were already treating a couple of the lightly wounded civilians when a small child was carried in.

The boy was only about a year old, and we were told he had been hit by some shrapnel either from a mortar or a B-40 rocket. Not that it mat-

"A-331" painted on camp roof for easy aircraft identification.

tered—shrapnel was shrapnel. The boy's lips were starting to turn blue and he was barely breathing. Doc' scooped him up and carried him to the operating room. He laid him on his back on the operating table and immediately began CPR. He shouted at me, *"Bac Si,* find the smallest airway tube you can and start bagging him."

I found a small airway tube, inserted it into the boy's throat, and attached an air bag to it. I began to "bag him," that is, to force air into his tiny lungs. He continued to lie on the operating table with Doc' pushing on his chest performing CPR and me bagging him over and over and over again. Doc' yelled at me above the din coming from the dispensary, "I can't see any bleeding. Do you see any?"

I kept bagging the boy with one hand and with my free hand began to examine his arms, legs, and the rest of him. He had no visible major wounds and there was no blood flow at all coming from his body. He should have been bleeding from somewhere but he wasn't. I couldn't find anything.

I yelled back at Doc', "I don't see any bleeding anywhere."

We were getting nowhere. The child was not responding. Still we kept going, not wanting to lose him. We continued to perform CPR, with Doc' pressing on his chest and me forcing air into his lungs, all the while trying to detect any type of a pulse.

The boy's lips were completely blue and his body looked lifeless. After 10 minutes I knew it was not good. But even though there was almost no chance of recovery we kept on trying to bring him back. After another five minutes I realized it was hopeless.

I stopped bagging the child and put my arms around Doc'. I embraced him and said, "Doc' it's over."

"I know, but we tried," he said with great sorrow in his voice.

We stopped and looked down at the now lifeless little body. I said a brief, silent prayer with tears in my eyes. I avoided eye contact with Doc' so as not to embarrass myself but it seemed to me like he was welling up also.

We went out to check on the others. None of the other villagers were hurt badly, only a few minor shrapnel injuries from the mortar fire. The CID medics had things under control and were treating and bandaging the wounds. Doc' and I supervised things until every one of the civilians from Loc Ninh had been taken care of and then we went back to the team room. I reflected on how the first casualty I had treated in Vietnam wasn't even old enough to walk or talk and there was nothing I could do to save him. A young, innocent victim.

Welcome to the war.

CHAPTER **3**

FIRST CONTACT

W ITHIN A WEEK OF arriving at Loc Ninh in May 1968, I was scheduled to go on a five-day, multi-company operation with Lieutenant
James Hunt, the Team's executive officer. I was the most junior team member in the camp, having been in-country for less than a month, while Lieutenant Hunt had been at Loc Ninh for six months. A senior person
in-country was always paired with a junior in-country, with the exception
that you could never go out with someone in your same MOS (Military
Occupational Specialty)—meaning two medics would never be on a mission together. But Lieutenant Hunt was the XO so it was okay for us to be
paired up together. A junior in-country was never in charge of an operation
even though he might outrank the senior in-country team member. This
was not a hard and fast rule but it was usually applied.

However, in this case it didn't matter, as Lieutenant Hunt outranked
me and had been in-country a lot longer. It did happen to me once later
on in my tour when I was paired up with a new in-country 2nd lieutenant.
While he was technically in charge because he outranked me, I was given
a wink and a nod with the understanding that I was to make sure everything ran smoothly.

The night before we went out on the operation we had a briefing in
the Intelligence Room. One wall of Intel consisted of a huge map of our
area of operations with all sorts of markers indicating reports of enemy
units and troop strengths. Unless the door was closed for briefings or up-
dates, the map was always covered by red curtains.

The commanding officer, Lieutenant Floyd Watson, and team sergeant
SFC Howard Hill, went over the mission objective with Hunt and me and

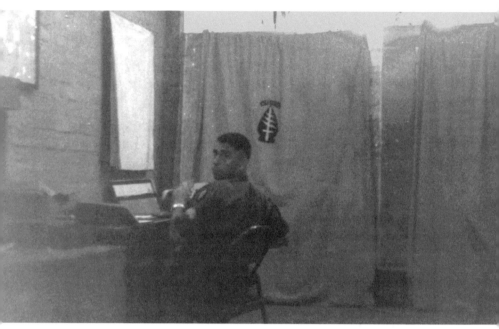

Intelligence room with red curtains drawn over intelligence maps on the wall.

the LLDB who would be with us. We were to patrol the eastern part of the AO, south of the old east-west Highway 14 which ran from Village 5 to the north of us, to the district of Bu Dop, to the east of us. Most of the patrol would be in the jungle east of the rubber plantation. There were intelligence reports of NVA infiltration coming from Cambodia and passing through the area while heading south along a route that ran just east of Village 10, a known VC village at the far eastern edge of our AO. We were to proceed east from Loc Ninh through the rubber plantation for approximately six miles, continue eastward through the jungle for another four miles, and then turn north to check out Village 10 and the area to the east of it.

On a five-day mission you carried everything with you—ammo, canteens, food, poncho, hammock, blanket, toilet paper, toothbrush, etc.— in a backpack or on an ammo belt. There was no re-supply in the field and if you needed something you had to bring it with you. The night before the mission the troops were issued five days of rations and ammo. I went to the supply room and procured a hammock but it was only about five feet long and obviously made for Vietnamese troops. Along with the hammock I got extra ammo, another canteen, and additional C rations.

I spoke to Lieutenant Hunt who said, "When we get back in, get another hammock from supply and there's a lady in Loc Ninh who will sew them together to make a bigger hammock for you."

I did not have a camouflage hat to wear so I borrowed one from Sp5 Burkett.

The US Special Forces team members all carried M-16's as did our counterpart LLDBs, members of the Vietnamese Special Forces. But the CID troops had only M-1's, M-1 carbines, a couple of M-2 carbines, and a BAR (Browning automatic rifle) or two. The only machine guns we had were old 30 caliber A-4's or A-6's and they were too heavy to carry in the field. The CIDs basically had weapons from World War II and Korea. We did not get M-16's or M-60 machine guns issued to our CIDs until halfway into my tour. The BAR's were not feasible for our troops to carry as they were almost as long as our people were tall.

Every time Lieutenant Hunt went out on a mission he always brought along an M-60 mortar and a mortar crew though no one else ever did this. I guess it was his thing.

The next day at dawn we met up with the troops who were assembled in the camp, and set out in combat formation heading east through the rubber plantation. After a six-mile hike through the rubber trees we stopped at the edge of the jungle for a break. I had never seen a jungle before except in pictures. In fact, I did not even know anyone who had ever seen or been in the jungle before. When I was young and growing up in northern Michigan I used to play in the woods all the time. The trees in Michigan were tall and the ground beneath them was usually covered with fallen branches and rotting logs. Ferns and weeds grew between the trees but you could still run in the woods by dodging the trees and forest debris while crashing through the foliage.

The jungle was different. It had tall and medium-sized trees but from the ground up, high weeds and vines grew everywhere—it was like being in a maze. You could not run through the jungle. You could not walk through it. You could not take even one step without the vines and thick weeds impeding you. And since the person on point had to cut and slash a path through the vegetation for the rest of us to follow, it was tough going.

It took at least an hour to advance one klick (kilometer), or a little over half a mile. We stopped every two hours to take a break and then again at noon so the troops could eat and rest. It was very difficult making our way through the jungle and eventually we were all exhausted. Especially me. Because they were only about 5 feet tall, the Vietnamese troops could easily stoop under branches and vines in the cut path, but at five-ten I had to duck down most of the time. It seemed like every branch, every weed, and every vine tried to push against me and snag my M-16, or my backpack, or my ammo webbing.

Around 4:30 we stopped to cook dinner. After everyone was done eating and relieving themselves we moved a little farther east to bed down. We did not want any bad guys to get too good a fix on our location for the night, even though it was the middle of the jungle.

The vegetation where we stopped for the night was not as dense. There were a lot of small trees and bamboo, but you could see at least five feet in every direction. The troops set up a defensive perimeter in a big circle with Lieutenant Hunt, the headquarters platoon, and myself in the center. To go to the bathroom you had to carry your weapon and go outside the circle. It was mostly a respect thing. You did not want to sleep near or take a chance of stepping in somebody's business. When I went to relieve myself, I carried my M-16 and made sure that everyone nearby saw me going out. I did not want to get shot by mistake when coming back in.

The troops were all setting up their hammocks by tying them between two trees or shrubs. When I tied mine up and tried to climb in, the shrubs it was tied to kept bending over, with the result that I would end up lying on the ground on top of the hammock. I finally found two sturdy little trees that would support my weight, but since the hammock was only five feet long my feet dangled out. It was not comfortable at all.

The next trick was to take the poncho and tie one corner of it to the tree at the foot end of the hammock and the opposite corner to the tree at the head end. With the poncho then tied about two feet over the hammock, it made a nice little tent. This would keep any dew or light rain off me during the night. Though both the temperature and humidity during the day were in the 90's, during the night it cooled down to the 70's or so, and was very damp. Lying in the hammock with the poncho tent overhead and a poncho liner for a blanket, I had no problem sleeping except for one thing. I didn't know what kind of wildlife to expect in the jungle: lions, tigers, elephants, snakes, monkeys. But there wasn't any. I asked Lieutenant Hunt about it and he said, "All the bombing and artillery have driven the wildlife up into Cambodia."

I wasn't sure if his explanation was true but it sounded reasonable enough. One time during my tour I did see a large ten-foot snake slither by and another time I spotted a small mule deer, but mostly the jungle was either empty of wildlife or the wildlife stayed well hidden. At night there were all sorts of sounds. The biggest noise maker was a tree frog that made a sound like, "Faak-you, Faak-you," and typically there must have been hundreds of them within earshot. Of course, we aptly named them "F*** You Frogs." But once I got accustomed to their nocturnal croaking, I was able to go to sleep.

During one of our operations we found a troop of small spider monkeys in the trees. The CIDs captured a baby monkey from the troop and brought it back to camp. Since it was an orphan, we adopted the baby monkey as a team mascot. We knew it was an orphan because the CIDs had eaten its mother.

Team mascot, Duk the monkey.

The next morning everyone had breakfast—the CIDs ate rice as they always did. We then moved out to the east through the jungle and swung to the north on the east side of Village 10, the VC village. We stopped on a small rise in a grove of medium-sized trees where we could look down on it.

Village 10 had only two roads, both just wide dirt paths. We could see down the length of the main road, which had maybe 15 thatched huts on each side, until it intersected and formed a 'T' with the north/south road.

Once again we stopped to eat. Lieutenant Hunt was showing me how to light small balls of C-4 and place them under a canteen cup to heat up lunch. He always carried a half stick of C-4 for cooking. You had to be careful as the stuff was highly explosive and burned extremely hot. I was just getting the hang of it when the troops all started whispering, "VC! *Beaucoup* VC!"

I dropped everything and grabbed my M-16. The CIDs were crouched behind trees and pointing toward the village. I got down behind a tree and spied seven or eight black pajama-clad VC walking on the road, coming straight toward us. The VC did not see us, and instead just waltzed along through the village like they owned it. Each of them carried an AK-47. The CIDs remained hidden behind trees as the VC kept getting closer.

Lieutenant Hunt was whispering orders to the mortar team to get set up when the shooting started. I don't know who shot first. The noise was deafening—all the CIDs were firing at the VC with every weapon they had and the VC were firing back with their AK's on full-automatic. I could not fire my M-16 as the CIDs were between me and the enemy, and I would have probably hit one of our own if I had done so. I started to move forward, running from behind one tree to the next, until I was on the front line of the CIDs.

The VC were firing and falling back while the CIDs continued shooting up the whole village, because the enemy was using the huts along the road as cover for their retreat. By the time Lieutenant Hunt was able to get some mortar rounds off, the VC had moved back to the "T" in the road. He and the crew put five rounds into the area. Then all was quiet—the enemy had run off and the CIDs had quit shooting.

Lieutenant Hunt was standing next to me, having just suddenly appeared. Amid all the excitement and gunfire I hadn't seen him since he was

A café in the village of Loc Ninh.

getting the mortar crew set up, but he now had his backpack on and said to me, "Let's get the CIDs to move out and sweep the village!"

I ran back, grabbed my stuff and put on my backpack. I picked up the camo hat that had fallen off in the mad scramble and noticed that it had landed on my little C-4 ball of fire, which burned a hole into the brim. All I could think was, "Burkett is going to be pissed because I put a hole in his hat."

Hunt took over and got the troops into formation and we swept through the village. As we approached the "T" in the road, we realized the VC were long gone, having run off to hide in the nearby jungle. A couple of elderly women from the village did have some minor shrapnel wounds from the mortar fire, but no one else was hurt. The CID medics bandaged their wounds and told them to go to Village 5 for further treatment. As far as we could tell, the VC all got away intact. It was something of a miracle that none of them were killed or seriously wounded—I thought surely a couple of them must have got hit from our gunfire and mortar rounds, but we could not find any bodies or blood trails.

My first "contact" with the enemy and I had not even fired my weapon. It all happened so fast: by the time I had taken cover, then moved up from one tree to the next, then come on line with the CIDs, it was all over.

We checked out the village and talked to the residents who all claimed, "No VC here, no VC here."

Lieutenant Hunt told me, "That's a lie; they had to know the bad guys who were walking through their village."

We then headed north and circled back to the west to see if we could discover where the enemy had run off, but we never did find them. The next three days were pretty boring—just walking through the woods and jungle and not spotting anything or anyone. On the fifth day around noon, we rolled into the village of Loc Ninh and stopped to grab lunch at a local open-air cafe. I bought a Coke for myself and one for my radio man, which tasted unusually good, a result of being out in the heat and the jungle for five days. We rested and drank our Cokes then walked the half mile back to camp and reported in.

Even though I had not fired my M-16 that day near Village 10, according to the Army I had been involved in a combat action. The VC were shooting at us and we were shooting back at them and it didn't matter that I did not get a shot off. Based on this combat action against the enemy, I was awarded a United States Army "Combat Medical Badge" (CMB). I was awarded the CMB because my MOS was Medical; it made no difference that I was not actually functioning as a medic on the operation. Otherwise, I would have been awarded the "Combat Infantry Badge" (CIB).

CHAPTER 4

RUNNING THROUGH RUBBER

I HAD BEEN IN-COUNTRY for approximately a month when SFC Howard Hill and I were out on a five-day, multi-company-sized operation. We started out going east, through the Village of Loc Ninh and into the rubber plantation. When we reached the jungle we turned north and roughly followed the line of rubber trees. We poked around for a couple of days in this area and did not see any action or observe any signs of enemy activity or movement. On a circular route back to camp we stopped at Village 5, approximately three miles north of Loc Ninh. Village 5 consisted of about 20 main buildings on Highway 13, with a few scattered houses off the main road. There was a small RFPF outpost on the east side of Highway 13.

Hill told me, "It's always good to stop in at Village 5 to show the flag"— that is, letting the inhabitants know that we were around and there for them.

We then proceeded westerly through the rubber plantation, planning to head south and back toward camp. Two miles west of Village 5 we swept through a tiny village of maybe 20 straw huts with thatched roofs and walls. We were not especially apprehensive during the sweep, as it was not a known VC village; most of its residents worked on the plantation tapping the rubber trees for sap. It was a nice quiet little spot so we stopped to eat lunch. There was even a well where we refilled our canteens.

The troops chatted with the residents, and seemed to be acquainted with many of them. This was my first time in the village and it was my understanding that our operations had not been here for six months or so. On the main trail through the village was a mini general store with a few items displayed on two tables in front, including loaves of fresh baked French bread.

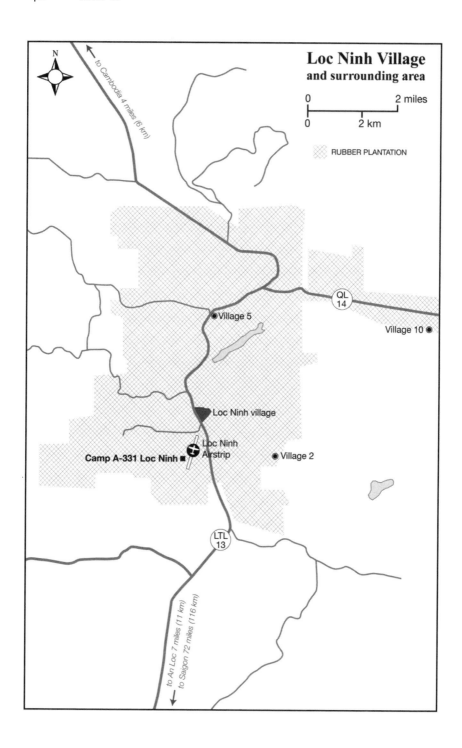

By this time I could count in Vietnamese up to ten, and I kept saying, "*mot*" (one in Vietnamese) and pointing to the loaves of bread, but the little old lady shopkeeper kept saying, "No, no, *hai*," (two in Vietnamese) and pointing to the bread. I only wanted one but for some reason you had to buy two. I gave the second loaf to my radio man.

The fresh bread was a nice welcome to my lunch, which consisted of a handful of rice boiled in water in a canteen cup over little lighted balls of C-4. The little balls of C-4 heated the rice up in no time at all. We always had a problem with claymore mines around the camp because the indigenous troops would steal the C-4 out of them to heat up their food. I now carried a quarter stick of C-4 on each mission to heat my rations.

While we were eating lunch, some of the workers who had come in from the rubber plantation for lunch said that they heard "*beaucoup* chopping" in the jungle due west of the village. The CID company commander talked with them further but all he could get was "*beaucoup* chopping." Even though I could count in Vietnamese up to 10 and had an understanding of the numbers past ten, everything with the troops was always "*beaucoup*" for a lot, or "*titi*" for a few. They probably assumed we could speak French because we were Caucasian and looked French enough to them.

The chopping was more than likely the NVA building a bunker complex. First they would dig a 6- by 6-foot hole about 5-feet deep, then place logs on top and cover it with dirt. A bunker like this would be a good place to be if you were getting shelled by artillery. Since this "*beaucoup* chopping" report sounded like a hot lead and not some vague piece of intelligence, we decided to go and check it out. Hill radioed back to the camp and gave them our situation and told them that we were going to investigate the chopping.

We moved out of the village in our standard three-column formation with one company on the right, one company on the left. The middle column consisted of a point platoon, a headquarters platoon behind them, and a rear platoon. This formation facilitated easy movement through the rubber plantation, as the rubber trees were all in neat rows roughly 20 feet apart. As we approached the edge of the plantation and could distinctly hear chopping sounds, the troops moved into a single rank. We advanced slowly forward toward the jungle. I was on the left flank with 15 CIDs to my left and SFC Hill was two rubber trees to my right with the rest of the troops on his right.

All at once, the middle of the formation started receiving AK-47 gunfire from the jungle; we must have jumped the enemy's forward position. Everyone immediately opened up and was returning fire. It was a hell of a racket with all of the CIDs shooting and the NVA shooting back at us.

At first I did not see any bad guys and then they were right in front of me, doing squad maneuvers to flank us on our left at the end of the formation. A squad maneuver is when half of the squad fires while the other half moves forward. Then the half of the squad that moved forward begins firing and the half that was firing moves forward. It is a very effective maneuver for advancing on or out-flanking an opposing force. *And they were doing it to us!* It certainly looked like we were up against some well-trained and disciplined NVA soldiers. I was shooting at a couple of them who were about 40 yards in front of me while yelling at the troops on my left to advance. Instead, the CIDs were trying to back off and retreat out of harm's way. If they kept backing off, the NVA would successfully flank our formation on the left and have us caught in a cross fire. And if that happened we would probably get wiped out.

Now we started to take heavy fire. The rubber trees were being ripped apart by the AK-47 rounds. The sap from the rubber tree I was standing behind dripped and splattered all over me as the rounds shredded its trunk.

I knew we could not let the NVA flank us so I screamed at the CIDs, *"Di, di!"* (Go, go!) and motioned them forward.

They screamed back at me, *"Beaucoup VC! VC caca dau!"* (meaning "the VC will kill us!")

I cursed at them and made references to their mothers and pointed my M-16 at them. I yelled, *"Di—di!"* and *"Bac Si (me) you caca dau!"* With more cursing and swearing at the CIDs on my left, and them cursing and swearing back at me, we managed to move up two to three rubber trees closer to the jungle and had for the moment cut off the NVA's flanking maneuver.

While all of this was going on, SFC Hill, who was still to my right, was firing at the advancing NVA while talking on the radio to the camp and reporting the contact. Hill then shouted at me, "I need a grenade!" A couple of NVA were 30 yards in front of him. They were behind a rubber tree and lying in a small ditch but kept popping up and shooting at us. Hill wanted a grenade to blow them out of their hiding hole.

I was about to yell back that I didn't have a grenade when 10 to 12 B-40 rockets, fired from RPG (rocket propelled grenade) launchers, exploded further to our right along the main line of our troops. Five seconds later there were another five or six B-40 rocket explosions and then another 10 to 12 explosions a few seconds after that. Each NVA squad usually had one RPG-7, and judging from the number of rockets fired at us in something like five seconds, we were directly facing two NVA companies.

We had stumbled onto an enemy battalion of possibly 500 dug in troops and we were about 150 in total. We were outmatched and outgunned. The whole tree line to our right came alive with intense AK-47 fire as the enemy massed for a charge.

Our troops had had enough. It was obvious that there were a whole lot more bad guys than there were of us. To a man, the CIDs took off running back the way they'd come. And when the troops take off and run, the officers don't have much choice but to follow them the hell out of the area, because there is nothing that can be done to convince them to stay and fight and die.

Moments later SFC Hill and I took off and were right on their tails, trying to catch up to them, but I guess we got a late start or the CIDs were faster because they remained some 50 yards ahead of us. We could not catch up. We were all running for our lives. Hill was about 10 feet in front of me and yelling on the radio trying to get some help—artillery, helicopter gunships, or anything. Bullets cracked over our heads, struck the ground behind us, and hit the trees around us. As the last man on the great retreat, I was trying to make sure that none of the bad guys caught up to us, and was also protecting Hill's back while he was on the radio. My radio man was nowhere to be found. He had bolted with the rest of the troops and was probably way ahead of us.

Our mad dash out of there must have taken the NVA by surprise, as they were busy using their military training to engage, flank, charge, and eliminate an opposing force. It probably gave their commanders a short pause once they realized we had fled the scene and they now had to figure out how to regroup and pursue us. But that was the break we needed. No one came after us.

I had been too busy covering the rear to realize exactly where we were running to. I only knew we were running through the rubber plantation in a generally eastward direction. Hill and I must have been pretty good runners after all, because we finally caught up with the troops before we approached Village 5, which was almost six klicks (three to four miles) from where we had started.

The whole time we were running Hill kept trying to get us some support. But we were moving too fast to figure out exactly where to call in artillery, and the rubber trees were so tall they blocked out any smoke grenades that we could have popped. Unless aircraft could identify our smoke and thereby our location, they would have had as good a chance of hitting us as the bad guys, and would not fire. Looking back on it, we should have called in artillery on the bunker complex that the NVA was constructing, but at that moment we just wanted to get them off our back and to survive.

We entered Village 5, which was roughly three miles north of Loch Ninh. Village 5 had a small contingent of RFPF's stationed there, so we all felt a little safer. We positioned the troops around the village and I sat down to catch a blow. I remember sitting on the front steps of a building on the main street of the village and having trouble lighting a cigarette because both my hands were shaking so bad, until I realized I already had

Company-sized operation leaving camp; CIDG barracks and tank are in the background.

a lit one going in my left hand. So much for calm, steady nerves.

This all happened on the fourth day of a five-day patrol. I began to check on the wounded, and besides a few minor shrapnel wounds from the B-40 rockets, everyone was in one piece and alive. One CID had a piece of shrapnel in his eye and would have to be medevac'd later, but it was a miracle that no one was hit more seriously.

While I was doing this, Hill was in touch with the camp and informed them we were out of ammo and needed either a re-supply or help in getting back. While they were running, the CIDs had dumped their backpacks and extra ammo—everything but their weapons. If the enemy had decided to pursue us, we would have been annihilated. Hill learned that while we were out in the field, the 11th Cavalry had arrived at Loch Ninh and was sitting at the end of the airstrip. The camp gave them the word so they mounted up to come to Village 5 and rescue us.

It had been quiet for maybe 15 minutes when we began to receive some probing fire from the rubber trees on the west side of the village. The NVA bastards had regrouped and followed us and were now setting up at the edge of the village getting ready to move in for the kill. And we had no way to defend ourselves.

Just as Hill and I were going to investigate what was going on we

Last of the operation leaving camp through the front gate; dispensary is in the background on the right.

heard a rumble coming up the road from Loch Ninh. It was the 11th Cav, with tanks and armored personnel carriers (APC's) coming up to help us. They rolled into the village and went on line at its western edge near the rubber trees, then opened up on the NVA and mowed them down. The 11th Cav chased the NVA through the rubber plantation and back to the bunkers they had been constructing, and then into the jungle.

It was now the NVA's turn to retreat and they ran for their lives, but the 11th Cav wiped them out every step of the way. The NVA infantry was no match for tanks and APC's. In their pursuit of us, they had probably become overconfident of their abilities and a little disorganized. They were definitely not expecting to go up against an armored force.

Thank you 11th Cav for saving my life. I don't remember which troop it was, as A, B, C, and D troops had all operated out of our camp at Loch Ninh. The 11th Cav also brought with them a deuce-and-a-half loaded with extra ammo so we could rearm our troops and make it safely back to camp.

As things turned out we had done our job! Our main mission objective in the field was to gather and report intelligence on enemy strength and locations and engage them if the opportunity presented itself. The opportunity presented itself, we engaged them, and we were able (lucky enough) to get support and put a real hurt on them. We had made contact with an NVA battalion-size force of up to 500 hardcore troops and lived to talk about it.

SFC Hill and I were recommended for the Bronze Star for this action. I don't know if he ever received his medal. I know that I didn't.

CHAPTER 5

RIGHT THERE

————————————

I WAS ON A FIVE-DAY, multi-company operation with SFC Harvey Pipes. Harv was the senior weapons specialist on A-Team 331. Our mission was to go up to the northern part of our AO and recon for enemy troop movement in the vicinity of a small Montagnard village approximately two klicks south of the Cambodian border. We were also supposed to check out Intel reports of an NVA hospital in the jungle just inside Cambodia with a Russian doctor who had recently gone to the village and vaccinated everyone for smallpox.

Now, Harv was a true professional soldier who only wanted to get out there in the field and kill some commies. Rumor had it that this was his third or fourth tour of Vietnam and each of the previous times he came home involuntarily after being wounded. I never had the courage to ask him about it, as it didn't seem like a topic for conversation. In my eyes he was a bigger-than-life hero and I wanted to somehow measure up to him and gain his approval.

The standard-issue uniform for going out on patrol was camouflaged jungle fatigues, jungle boots, and a cloth camouflaged hat. But Harv always took his green beret along with him. Once he cleared eyeshot of the camp he would take off the camo hat and put on his beret. This was the first time that Harv and I had gone out on a mission together and he told me the night before, "I'm taking my beret with me and you can do what you want to do." I did not want to disappoint Harv so I packed my beret in my backpack to take on patrol. I had only been in-country for a couple months and was still unsure if I had what it took to do the job. To be a good soldier and to react and fight properly and not be afraid is something you don't know you can do until you have experienced combat a few times. The next morning we met up with our troops, who were assembled in formation, and went out the front gate heading east. And sure enough, as soon as we had gone a short distance from the camp, Harv put on his beret.

I got mine out and put it on too.

Once we were in the rubber plantation we turned north, taking a back way into Village 5. After a brief rest we continued traveling north by a sort of roundabout way, thinking it would keep anyone in the village from knowing exactly where we were going. There were always Vietnamese around who were sympathetic to the Viet Cong and wouldn't hesitate to give away our location, direction, and/or objective if they could. The first night we camped out in the rubber plantation north and east of Village 5 and planned to go to the Montagnard village the first thing in the morning.

Early the next day we approached the village. We set up on two sides of it in an L-shaped formation with one side moving through the village and the other side providing cover. The village consisted of 30 or so thatched huts sitting on top of five-foot high poles. We completed the sweep and did not find any bad guys, only some old men and women and children. All of the young men were gone.

Once the village was secured, the other half of our troops came in and the CIDs spoke to the residents. Some of our 'Yard troops knew the residents of the village and it was like old-home week for them. An older woman, probably in her forties but looking about eighty, came up and started to talk to them. She told them that her son was nearby and wanted to surrender to us. She said that he had been a CID from our camp at Loc Ninh, but when he came home on leave a couple of years ago, the VC came to the village and made him join up with them. Some of the troops recognized his name and remembered him, so the CID company commander told her to go and get him and he would be welcomed back. The Montagnard lady scurried off and in a few minutes returned with her son who had been hiding in the jungle nearby.

As the CID company commander talked to him and verified his story, the young 'Yard started talking. We were interested in just gathering some basic intelligence but he was telling all. He related that the VC came through the village when he was home on leave and basically drafted him, but they would not let him carry or use a weapon. Instead, they made him haul large bags of rice the whole time. He said he wanted to join back up with us so he could carry a weapon and because our pay of roughly 30 dollars a month was a whole lot more than what the VC were paying him.

He was very chatty and happy to be back with us. For one thing, all Vietnamese—North or South—hated the Montagnards and considered them subhuman. The arrangement we had with our troops was that they were all treated the same and were all paid the same whether they were Vietnamese, Montagnard, Cambodian, or Khrum Kampuchea Khmer.

As the 'Yard was talking we were trying to get him to tell us where he had been when he was carrying the rice. This was not very easy, as our interpreter was a Vietnamese who spoke only a little of the Montagnard language, and the 'Yard spoke only a little Vietnamese. To top it off, not only could he not read and write, he really could not even count.

He told us that it was "a *beaucoup* camp of VC." Of course, VC could mean anything from a ragtag group of locals to a hard-core NVA unit. Trying to get him to show us on a map the location of the camp was pointless, as he did not comprehend the concept of a map. The best we could get from him was that it was "a half-day's walk that way," and he pointed to the south. After further questioning it was determined that the half-day walk was more like, "walk in morning 'til eat lunch." Harv radioed this in and we were told to change our mission and have the 'Yard lead us to the alleged VC encampment. We were only in the second day of our mission with plenty of supplies and ammo and were good to go. It was around 9 AM as we set off.

We followed the 'Yard as he lead us south through the jungle along small trails. The trails skirted the rubber plantation, which was off to our right. After three hours we crossed a major east-west path that I knew was slightly east of Village 2, a known VC village. We crossed the path and were still heading south. The jungle here wasn't very thick and there were even a few open areas four to five feet wide. I was on the left flank with 10 CIDs ahead of me. Harv was about 20 feet to my right following the CID company commander, a point squad, and the 'Yard who was guiding us.

The CID commander stopped and asked the 'Yard, "How much farther is it to the VC?"

The Yard pointed directly ahead of us and said, "Right there."

And at that moment, all hell broke loose "right there" in front of us, with AK-47 gunfire, machine gun fire, and RPGs aimed at the point squad and the CID company commander in front of Harv. We had walked right up to the VC camp, which was actually NVA. The entire squad was down and so was the commander. The CIDs in front of me and the ones standing in front of Harv started to run away. Harv yelled to me, "Cover me *Bac Si!*" as he was firing straight ahead at the bad guys. Just then, two CIDs with an M-60 machine gun tried to run past me. I grabbed them both and sat them down, with Harv still yelling at me, "God damn it, cover me!"

I shouted back at Harv, "Let me get the 60 set up!"

The CIDs I had grabbed started to fire the machine gun. The M-60 cut down everything in front of us and Harv again yelled, "God damn it, cover me *Bac Si!*"

I shouted back at Harv, "I got ya covered!" I stood right next to the M-60 and unloaded clip after clip on full-automatic from my M-16, shooting from my hip in the direction of the bad guys. It didn't matter that I was standing in the open. I was covering Harv no matter what. He moved forward and got ahold of two wounded point squad CIDs and began dragging them, one in each hand, to the rear. On Harv's second trip to recover the wounded, some of the CIDs on the right, who had not run but were hiding with their heads down, started to provide him additional cover fire. He made at least three trips and recovered everyone who was down.

Some CIDs helped carry the wounded back from where Harv had dragged them, something I didn't notice at the time—I was too busy blasting everything in front of me and making sure that the two CIDs with the M-60 kept firing and did not cut and run. I never did see any of the enemy, but the M-60 guys and I made them keep their heads down, which allowed Harv to get the wounded out of there. The CIDs, Harv, and I backed out of the area toward the main east-west trail we had previously crossed, all the while firing in the direction of the bad guys. Harv got on the radio and called in the "contact" to our camp and got two ARVN 105mm howitzers to begin shelling the NVA camp to cover us. We then backed onto the main trail and headed toward the edge of the rubber plantation in the direction of Loc Ninh. Once on the trail we called in air strikes on the NVA position and the whole area, which we had just withdrawn from, exploded from all the ordnance being dropped on it.

Between the jungle and the rubber trees there was an open area big enough to get a medevac chopper in for our wounded. We convinced the chopper to land and put the severely wounded on it and they were off to a field hospital. Once we had them out of there, we headed back to camp because we were out of ammo, had some walking wounded, and were pretty much spent. Amazingly, the young 'Yard who led us right up to the bad guys did not have a scratch on him even though everyone around him had been hit.

On the march back to camp we heard the 105's from Loc Ninh pounding the NVA encampment. There then came a lull followed by a major air strike then another air strike and then another. The jungle behind us was being obliterated. Later that day the 11th Cav, who were operating in our AO, attacked with tanks and APC's and swept them up.

Again, we had done our job. We had located the enemy and put a major hurt on him. Not by engaging them with small arms fire but by finding them and being able to call in artillery and air strikes on their position, thus enabling the 11th Cav to go in and wipe them out. Intelligence reports the next week indicated that the VC had rounded up entire villages in the outlying area to act as stretcher-bearers, to carry the dead and wounded north into Cambodia where, supposedly, the hospital with the Russian doctor was located. The casualty reports that I heard ranged from a couple hundred up to three thousand. There was no way to truly verify any number.

Our operation did sustain some severely wounded but luckily we did not lose anyone. One of the most badly injured was the Vietnamese CID company commander. He returned from the hospital a couple of months later, and upon his return a big party was held, with lots of eating and drinking. I was one of the guests of honor along with Harv. The CID commander toasted Harv and me for saving his life.

There was a great deal of drinking going on, and Nick, my Vietnamese interpreter, was so drunk that he could no longer interpret or speak English. He would try but it would be all slurred and then he would start to giggle and laugh. My Vietnamese was very poor. I could count, say hello, tell someone to come or go, make reference to their mother, and that was about it. At the party we were all drinking and eating some type of meat that I couldn't identify. I tried to get Nick to tell me what kind of meat it was but he was too far-gone and no one else understood a thing I was saying. I pointed at the meat and went "Moo, moo," and got no response; I again pointed at the meat and went, "Oink, oink."

The CIDs all looked confused until one of them finally understood what I was trying to clarify.

"No, no *Bac Si*—woof, woof."

I was eating dog! It hadn't tasted too bad until I knew what it was.

Interpreter Nick in front of mortar pit.

Interpreter Ahn in outer compound with CIDG barracks in background.

Years later, after American troops had left Vietnam and the NVA were beginning to finish off the South Vietnamese Army, there was a front-page picture and article in the newspaper showing the first NVA capture of a district headquarters. It was Loc Ninh. The picture showed the NVA soldiers standing on the airstrip and on the bunkers surrounding our camp. The article stated that the NVA had captured Loc Ninh, which was only four miles from their headquarters during the war. It had been in the jungle just to the east of us the whole time. It seems that Harv and I had found their headquarters and put a real smack down on them. It also explains why every time we went east of Village 2 into the jungle, we could count on having "contact" with the enemy.

CHAPTER 6

CHIEU HOI BY THE KKK

Chieu Hoi WAS AN initiative undertaken by US forces in conjunction with the South Vietnamese government. Roughly translated, it meant "open arms." The basic program was that if any North Vietnamese soldier or Viet Cong insurgent was to willingly surrender, he would be reimbursed financially and welcomed as a citizen, and face no punishment whatsoever. The payment for surrender was about 50 *dong*, and if the enemy combatant turned in a weapon he could receive more *dong* based on what type of weapon it was. At the time, one *dong* of South Vietnamese currency was equivalent to one American dollar, and the average wage in Vietnam was about 30 *dong* per month. So by surrendering, an NVA or a VC could get two or three months' worth of wages. Two other factors contributed to the success of the *Chieu Hoi* program. First, the pay of a South Vietnamese soldier, or even one of our CIDs at Loc Ninh, was at least 30 *dong* per month. This was three to four times what a member of the NVA or a Viet Cong was paid. Second, when I was in Vietnam, we were winning the war. Since the NVA/VC had expended all of its resources earlier in the year during the *Tet* offensive, we were now prevailing in all of the important battles. As a result, the number of *Chieu Hoi* defections greatly increased.

Another aspect of the program was that when one of our troops captured an AK-47, an SKS semi-automatic carbine, or a rocket-propelled grenade launcher (RPG)—all standard Soviet bloc weapons—he would be paid approximately 30 *dong* for it by someone on the Team. We took possession of the seized weapons to insure that they did not find their way onto the black market and back into the enemy's hands. Thus, we always had a stockpile of captured enemy weapons on hand.

On August 15, 1968, the A-Team at Loc Ninh was involved with one of the largest, if not the largest, *Chieu Hoi* defections of an *en masse* enemy force. Elements of the 166th KKK (Khrum Kampuchea Khmer) Regiment somehow got word to our B-Team at An Loc that they desired to surrender under the terms of the *Chieu Hoi* program. The KKK was a Cambodian military force that operated as border bandits between Vietnam and Cambodia, after being pushed out of Cambodia proper in the 1950's and 60's in a revolution that they lost. Since that time, they had been employed by the Viet Cong and the North Vietnamese Army as an active fighting force against the American and South Vietnamese armies. The NVA not only funded them, but supplied them with modern weapons. In return the KKK was expected to fight alongside the NVA.

When Lieutenant Colonel Donald Martin, our B-Team commander at An Loc, received the Intel that elements of the KKK wished to surrender, he kicked it upstairs to the C-Team level in Bien Hoa, to Lieutenant Colonel Malcomb Rhine. Within hours a plan was put into motion to facilitate the surrender. The 166th KKK Regiment had previously operated in our AO and was supposedly nearby, somewhere north and west of us in Cambodia. The plan was basically to use our company-size operation, already on patrol in the northern part of the AO and led by SFC Harvey Pipes and Sp4 William Hart, to secure an LZ (landing zone) where the LTC's would be waiting to meet up with the defecting KKK, commanded by a Colonel Bradith. The company would then escort them to Village 5.

In the meantime, 1st Lieutenant Robert Robinson, the Civic Affairs/ Psychological Operations Officer at A-331, would lead another operation to clear Route 13, the road between Loc Ninh and Village 5, and would be waiting there for the arrival of the KKK, along with the trucks that would transport them to our camp. Lieutenant Robinson's troops would also be available if the "meet and greet" didn't go well or ran into heavy enemy contact. One of the determining factors in the KKK's decision to surrender at Loc Ninh was that we already had a company of KKK as one of our five combat units. The KKK in our camp were probably closely related to those who wanted to surrender, and must have reassured them that they would receive fair treatment by A-Team 331.

While the KKK were comfortable in surrendering to us, we weren't comfortable with them. We didn't trust them one bit. They had long been

Lieutenant Robert Robinson, Civic Affairs / Psychological Operations Officer.

operating in our AO and fighting against us. In fact, less than a month before this, elements of the 166th regiment were involved in an action, along with the NVA, near Village 5, directed against one of our operations. Our team's XO, 1st Lieutenant Joseph Miller, was KIA and our young Vietnamese interpreter, Do Van Du, was severely wounded, losing an arm and a leg. In this action the KKK did not directly attack our troops but were used as a blocking force by the NVA. Still, as far as we were concerned, these guys were mercenaries fighting for whichever side paid them the most and best fit into their long range plans of taking over Cambodia.

"What if it's a trick?" many of us wondered back at the camp.

What if the NVA were using the KKK and paying them to set a trap for our troops who had been sent out to welcome them in? It was estimated that approximately 100 KKK were surrendering. The company led by Pipes and Hart was only about 125 CIDs. First Lieutenant Robinson led a force of similar size, leaving the camp with only three companies to defend itself. If one or both of the operations were to become engaged in contact with a large NVA force, and if the KKK did not really surrender but instead attacked our troops, we would not have the resources to properly reinforce our people in the field and still be able to defend the camp. Some believed that was the objective—to have us commit our troops outside of the camp, ambush them with a numerically superior force, and then overrun the A-331. We knew that for this operation we would not receive troop reinforcements from any other source that could be there and protect our back.

There would be, however, a Forward Air Control plane patrolling the general area where the rendezvous was to take place, which could coordinate air strikes if necessary. On our airstrip we saw two Cobra gunships sitting there that were dedicated to the operation, standing by to take off on a moment's notice to provide close air support. In addition, we had the two Vietnamese 105's pointed to the north and ready to fire, and the big 175mm guns at An Loc were likewise dialed into the situation and able to provide more artillery if needed. I even jumped into the mortar pit because SFC Pipes, the senior weapons man normally in charge of the mortars, was in the field and I wanted to assist in any way I could.

Fortunately the operation went well, with the KKK being directed into the prepared LZ via a note dropped to them from a helicopter, a prerecorded message broadcast from a small plane, and signal shots fired by our operation to give them the exact rendezvous location. Colonel Bradith and his men were greeted at the LZ by Lieutenant Colonels Martin and Rhine, who arrived by helicopter from Village 5, approximately 5 klicks away. The KKK were required to immediately surrender their ammunition but were allowed to keep their weapons for the time being. The ammo was then loaded onto a couple of other helicopters and flown out.

The FAC plane then reported that "a large unidentified unit of troops was moving toward the border on the trail of the KKK." Upon hearing that, the LTC's and Colonel Bradith boarded choppers and flew straight back to Loc Ninh. As the last of the helicopters was leaving, it was later reported that two gunshots were directed toward it, "presumably from advance scouts of an NVA unit that was hot on the trail" of the defectors. With our CIDs providing point, flank, and rear security, the KKK moved out and proceeded quickly through the rubber plantation toward Village 5. They made it safely to the village, got on board the trucks that were waiting for them, and without incident were convoyed to a temporary compound set up outside of our camp by the airstrip. Harv and Specialist Hart and the rest of the company followed them on foot. As we still did not trust these guys and did not want a repeat of the Trojan horse story, the temporary compound was surrounded by barbed wire and armed guards, and equipped with tents for eating, sleeping and bathing. The KKK were fed hot food, and cold drinks were made available.

A total of 95 had surrendered. While they were being fed and interrogated and were settling in for the night, I set up a small clinic to examine them and treat any medical problems. Aside from a few malaria cases and some minor scratches and wounds, they were pretty healthy for the most part, though they also looked very tired and underfed. While I didn't pay much attention to it until I finished treating them, I saw that their equipment, webbing, packs, etc., looked old and beat up. This group did not appear to be a well-equipped fighting force.

Later, as I was standing around the compound, one of my teammates came up to me and said, "Did you notice their weapons? They are all old French single-shot rifles from World War I. They don't have even one AK-47 or semi-automatic SKS with them."

As we gathered in the team room that night, Top, our team sergeant, told us, "The KKK had probably hidden all of their AK-47's, rocket launchers, and machine guns that the NVA furnished them with, to avoid having to turn them in and to save them for a later date. Wonder where the hell they even found all of those old rifles. They haven't been used in years. Crafty little bastards aren't they."

The next morning a couple of Caribou aircraft landed at our airstrip. We loaded up the KKK and they were off for their first airplane ride ever, to An Loc. I don't know whatever became of this group of KKK *Chieu Hoi's*—whether they were incorporated into a Vietnamese army unit or enlisted to serve with another A-Team. We sort of expected some of them to be assigned to us, as we had one of the very few KKK companies at an A-Team camp in Vietnam. But they were out of our hair so it didn't matter if we did not trust them.

The incident of the KKK *Chieu Hoi's* was written up in the October 1968 issue of *The Green Beret* magazine, in an article entitled "Green Berets Meet The KKK." I was even mentioned in the article though they misspelled my last name.

Overall, our team had participated in one of the largest *Chieu Hoi's* of the war and had performed our mission outstandingly. We were now recognized by the higher-ups as one of the best A-Teams in III Corps. But we also got some unwanted recognition. I guess by taking in Colonel Bradith and the KKK's of the 166th Regiment, we pissed off some bad guys. On August 19, 1968, only a few days after sending the *Chieu Hoi* KKK group off, our camp was hit with a surprise attack by a multi-regimental size force of NVA.

No more time to bask in the glory. The fight was on.

CHAPTER 7

BATTLE OF LOC NINH

O N AUGUST 19, 1968, Special Forces Camp A-331 at Loc Ninh, CTZ III, was attacked by a multi-regimental NVA force estimated to be between 5,000 and 7,000 strong. At that time we had on hand 11 US Special Forces personnel, including myself; approximately eight LLDB (Vietnamese Special Forces); and around 700 CIDG (Civilian Irregular Defense Group) troops.

The attack started in the middle of the night with a devastating mortar shelling that lasted for nearly an hour. The NVA mortar crews were very accurate as they walked their 82mm rounds across the camp and back again. The rounds would hit roughly 20 yards apart and blow up anyone or anything out in the open, and caused a great deal of destruction. At some point during the mortar barrage, the NVA ground assault came in human wave charges from the area just north of the camp, where the rubber trees were only a 100 yards or so distant from our outer perimeter.

As soon as the mortar shells started coming in, we began to return fire from our own mortar pits, where our pre-aimed and pre-charged mortar rounds were launched to specific locations around the camp's perimeter. We also launched the mortars with flares. These were likewise pre-charged and ready to fire, and used for illuminating the general area of the camp. The flares were attached to parachutes and would go up about 1,000 feet where the parachutes would deploy and the flare would ignite. This enabled us to observe the attacking enemy troops who would no longer be operating under cover of darkness.

Our CIDs were all in their defensive positions on the wall of the berm and in concrete machine gun bunkers. They fired on the charging NVA with machine guns and small arms fire. One of the basic camp defenses was the concertina barbed wire strung around the perimeter in two or three different loops. The loops were interlaced with still more strands of concertina wire configured into X shapes that extended from the berm to the outermost perimeter of barbed wire. Machine guns were placed in each of the bottom parts of the X, with their fire being directed along the crisscrossing lines of the X, thus yielding interlocking fields of fire. Enemy troops trying to penetrate the camp were slowed down by the X-shaped configurations of barbed wire, and caught in the resulting kill zones.

Well-disciplined CIDs on machine guns were able to inflict significant casualties on the attackers, if not stop their charges altogether. Riflemen were positioned to protect the machine gun crews from any stray NVA. Other riflemen were positioned along the berm primarily to clean up any of the enemy who survived the interlocking machine gun fire.

The fierce, initial assault by the NVA breached the outer wire and was threatening to penetrate the inner wire and the camp. The combination of mortar fire, interlocking machine gun fire from the concrete bunkers, and the use of two Vietnamese 105mm howitzers attached to our camp stopped the NVA for the moment.

Moment, I say—hell it went on all night long! They wanted to overrun us and kill us all. They continued probing and charging and would not relent. We did get additional fire support during the night from some Cobra helicopter gunships, an AC-130 gunship, and US artillery at An Loc. The AC-130 gunship was a converted C-130 transport aircraft mounted with miniguns and 20mm cannon. It could put one round in every square foot of an area the size of a football field in a short blast of gunfire. But even with all this fire power being unleashed on them, the NVA continued to attack.

At some point during the night (everything time-wise was and still is blurry) the main threat of being overrun was over and the mortar attack had let up. I took advantage of the lull and ran back to the main medical bunker. Two-thirds of the bunker was underground and the roof was reinforced by rails from an old French railroad and topped with sandbags. It could withstand a direct hit by almost anything the enemy had. It was a safe place to be during a mortar attack.

By now the CID medics were carrying their wounded comrades to the bunker because the camp dispensary was not safe. The dispensary was an above ground wood-frame building and any mortar hit could have taken it out. In fact one mortar round did penetrate the roof during the attack and exploded right in the pharmacy.

View of dispensary after being hit by mortar round, August 1968.

The medical bunker became the site of a mass casualty situation as the many severely wounded CIDs were being brought in. We sorted things out, with those in the worst condition who could be saved being given top priority, while the less seriously injured had to wait. No Special Forces soldiers or LLDBs had been hit. A couple of CIDs were KIA (Killed in Action) and had to be moved out of the bunker to make room for the WIA's (Wounded in Action) coming in. Another medic was working on a CID who had a severe abdominal wound and I started working on one who had a large sucking chest wound. I did not think that he was going to live so I put a dressing on his chest wound, gave him some morphine for pain, and rolled him on his wounded side to try to keep the good lung from filling up with blood. I then went on to treat a couple of other severely wounded CIDs who I thought had a better chance of making it. Between the CID medics, the three CID nurses, the other medic and myself, we were nearly overwhelmed with the situation. But no one panicked, we just worked. We were trained to save lives and that's what we did.

In the early morning light the medical bunker was a mess with blood and bloody gauze and bloody bandages all over the place. We had saved the more severely wounded, and the less severely wounded were now being patched up in the hallway by the CIDs. I was about to take a break and do what I don't know when I remembered the CID with the chest wound that I believed could not be saved. He was lying on his side on a stretcher in a corner of the bunker and was still alive.

Holy shit, that guy should be dead, I said to myself.

But he must have had a great amount of "will to live" because he was still with us. I immediately began to work on him. I had sacrificed him so that I could save two or three others, but he had hung on and was clinging to life. If he had that amount of will power, I was going to make sure that he made it. We all started to work on him now, patching the chest wound and aspirating the blood from the chest cavity. An officer, or maybe the team sergeant, came to check up on us and see how many wounded we had. He asked, "Are you going to need a medevac?"

I said, "We've got a full bird and need it ASAP. We have some critically wounded who need to get out of here and get to an operating room because there's nothing more we can do for them."

At this point we were still taking occasional mortar fire. The enemy would fire 10 or 20 rounds and walk them right across the camp. We were also taking sporadic gunfire from the rubber trees outside the perimeter. The only place we could land a medevac chopper was inside the compound, as we could not even think about trying to get to the airstrip, 50 yards east of the camp. The NVA were everywhere around us and would not respect a big Red Cross on a helicopter. To them it was just a target. If they shot any type of helicopter down, they would probably get some type of Ho Chi Minh medal.

Calling for a medevac, and actually getting one to land while we were taking incoming rounds, were two different things. The NVA remained massed in the area to the north of the camp. While not making any ground assaults on us at the moment, we suspected that they were dug in among the rubber trees, using them as cover to direct the mortar barrages.

I did not speak to the medevac pilot myself but it took a couple of hours to convince him to set the bird down in the camp, as the landing zone was, in helicopter terminology, a "hot LZ." The chopper finally landed during a brief letup from the mortars. We moved quickly to put the severely wounded CIDs on board and they were off to the hospital.

In the end, they all survived and returned to duty in a few months, including the fellow with the strongest will to live that I have ever seen—the CID with the terrible chest wound that I had set aside to die. We had only two KIA during that first night which is remarkable considering it was a sneak attack. We never suspected that we were going to get hit. I guess Intel missed all those multiple NVA regiments of over 5,000 troops sneaking right up to our doorstep.

For four more days we continued to take mortar fire during the day, and ground assaults and mortar fire at night. There were three more human wave attacks, but none of them as threatening as on that first night. We had lots of help now from the sky, with B-52's bombing the area between us and Cambodia. Cobra helicopter gunships continued strafing the area around the camp and there were nightly visits from "Puff the Magic Dragon," a propeller driven AC-47 gunship whose miniguns, when fired in the darkness, looked to be shooting "tongues of fire" at the enemy. In addition, we got all the fire support missions we wanted from the big guns down at An Loc.

On the fifth day I watched, from the berm of our outer defensive wall, an air strike on a couple of old French mansions. The French had long ago abandoned the mansions, which were approximately a half-mile away from camp. The NVA were holed up in there and probably using them as cover to call in mortar fire on us. The Air Force jets dropped their bombs directly on top of the mansions and destroyed them. They then flew toward our camp and went full-throttle straight up so all we could see was the fire coming out of their tail, accompanied by a loud roar from the engines. It was their sign off to us—mission accomplished.

Elements of the 11th Cav and the 1st Division were able to fight their way up Highway 13 from An Loc and set up at the end of the airstrip, which greatly relieved the pressure on us. The 1st Division had a major battle with the NVA in the rubber plantation to the north of camp during the next few days, and afterwards the enemy slipped back across the border into Cambodia.

They had failed to overrun us.

On the sixth day, I was on the first patrol that was able to leave camp and go outside the wire. We inspected the perimeter, not knowing if there were still any bad guys hanging around. We did not encounter any live ones but did find quite a few who had not made it, lying in ditches or in inaccessible areas. We did not have to look too hard either. We could tell where they were by the foul odor. Exposure to the 90-degree heat for a few days will cause a body to smell real bad.

The CIDs would not approach the dead bodies because they could not handle it. I did not have a problem, however. Sure they smelled bad but it did not bother me all that much. An instance that did bother me was when the CIDs had found a dead NVA soldier lying in a little opening in the weeds. As they stood back and held their noses, I approached and saw that the dead guy had a cool green pith helmet on. It looked to me like a great souvenir so I reached down to take it off of his head.

As I removed the helmet, I saw that the entire back of its inside was covered with his brain tissue. I dropped the helmet immediately. The CIDs were all standing there laughing at me and when I rejoined them they were saying that *Bac Si* was "*dinky-dau*," (crazy).

The NVA were usually very good about recovering their dead and wounded, but on our operation that day we found 20 to 30 bodies that were hidden from plain view. Another 88 bodies were entangled in the rolls of barbed concertina wire that surrounded the camp. They would be impossible to untangle from the wire and were by now getting very ripe. Some demo guys came around later and used diesel fuel to burn them in place.

Water tank truck hit by 75mm recoilless rifle, August 1968.

The attack did expose one major weakness. Our water supply was in the old camp, which was now the CIDs' dependents' housing, located a half-mile from the present camp. To get water under normal conditions, we had a water tanker truck go there a couple times a day and fill up. So not only did we not have a fresh supply of water during the assault, but the water tank on the truck was struck by a 75mm recoilless rifle shell and had a two-foot hole in it. A couple weeks later, after things had quieted down, some Army engineers arrived and dug a new well for us in the camp and took away our damaged tanker truck.

As I said earlier, much of what happened, especially the first night of the attack, is mostly a blur in my memory. I know it was a complete surprise attack and lasted most of the night and it was touch and go whether or not we were going to be overrun. But the initial assault by the NVA was turned back and we survived. After that the situation was not quite so dire.

Victory celebration following the attack of August 18–22;
Bac Si Cong and author walking to the party.

I came back to the States in May 1969 and processed out of the Army. In August 1970, while I was attending college, I received in the mail a Bronze Star Medal with a "V" for valor from the Army. The accompanying award citation read: *"For heroism in connection with ground operations against a hostile force in the Republic of Vietnam: Sergeant Krizan distinguished himself by heroism on August 19, 1969 while serving as a Special Forces Medic. During a multi-regimental attack on Loc Ninh Special Forces Camp by the NVA—*blah, blah, blah. . . ." The attack on the camp occurred in August 1968 but the award stated that the action occurred in August 1969 when I was already home.

So much for medals.

CHAPTER 8

LOC NINH, SEPTEMBER 1968

I N EARLY SEPTEMBER 1968 we received intelligence reports that a large body of NVA had crossed over from Cambodia and were in the jungle in the far eastern part of our AO that bordered Bu Dop. The intelligence reports put their numbers as somewhere between multiple regiments up to a full division. An NVA regiment consisted of three to four battalions of 300 to 350 soldiers each, and the total force was estimated to be around 5,000 hardcore enemy troops. Based on this intelligence, the 1st Division moved up to Loc Ninh.

The old French highway, Route 13, also known as "Thunder Road," ran straight north from Saigon, through An Loc and right up to Loc Ninh, then into Cambodia. The highway wasn't always safe, as the bad guys often set up ambushes on it, but an armored convoy could easily fight its way to Loc Ninh and keep the road open for re-supply. A-331 was a great place for an American operation to headquarter while operating in the field. We had an airstrip capable of handling C-130 cargo planes for re-supply, plenty of available LZ's for helicopters, and excellent defensive positions just off the western end of the airstrip.

Typically, American units would have an established base somewhere in the Saigon area where about one-fourth of their troops would remain with the headquarters unit. Another fourth would be deployed in the immediate area and charged with securing the base, while another fourth would be in the base camp resting or getting ready to go out into the field. The remaining fourth would be on an operation somewhere. When they did so, they came to places like Loc Ninh. For them it was their field trip; for me, it was my home for almost a year. I lived in the field.

We could always tell when a major American unit was going to move in because Vietnamese prostitutes would set up little tents in the rubber trees across from the airstrip a day or two ahead of time. The prostitutes' intelligence-gathering skills were excellent and probably a whole lot better than our own. We should have been using them for information, as they probably knew the location of the NVA better than we did. Guys will be guys.

True to form, the day after the prostitutes had set up their tents in the rubber trees on the other side of the airstrip, units of the 1st Division began to arrive. They bivouacked at the end of the airstrip and secured the entire surrounding area, as well as to the south of our camp. Trucks rumbled up and down the dirt road that paralleled the airstrip, while MPs (Military Police) directed the traffic. The troops prepared defensive fortifications to the south of the airstrip. Planes were constantly landing and delivering more men and supplies and the whole scene now looked like a major American military base.

We were not allowed to venture out of camp. The units of the regular Army were in charge and we were nothing but a bunch of ragtags to them. It was their operation and we were supposed to sit this one out. In fact, our CO was written up by American MPs for driving the team's jeep on the road to Loc Ninh that ran parallel to the air strip. Our own road!

My views on the early part of the battle between American forces and the NVA are not based on any hard cold facts but only on my observations and on the scuttlebutt and rumors that I heard, of which maybe 90% were true. Here is my understanding of what happened.

A recon patrol was sent out into the jungle in the eastern part of our AO to where the NVA force was thought to be. Once in the jungle the recon patrol was not heard from again. They had vanished, apparently wiped out by the NVA. A full-strength recon company was then sent out to investigate and they radioed back that they were in contact and were being cut to pieces and had sustained over 50% casualties. Now the fight was on. The rest of the American units sitting at the airstrip moved out to engage the enemy and were going toe to toe with them. We could stand on the berm of the outer defensive positions of our camp and see helicopters and fixed wing aircraft making gun runs on the bad guys in the jungle approximately six miles to the east of us. There was every type of aircraft available and they were shooting, rocketing, and dropping bombs on the enemy positions.

As we watched the helicopters in the distance, it looked like not all of them were coming back up after making their gun runs—and they weren't. The NVA forces included an antiaircraft battalion. Their antiaircraft weapons were quad .51 caliber machine guns and they must have had nearly a dozen of them. With four .51 caliber machine guns all firing at once at a single target they were shooting down our helicopters in great numbers. There was a report that a helicopter carrying a general from the 1st Division was hit during the day and crashed as it flew over the battlefield and all on board were lost. The battle went on all day but quieted down that night as the Americans dug in. During this time there were probing operations by the NVA, attempting to overrun American positions in the jungle.

The next day the battle began in earnest again. The Americans bombed the entire area repeatedly and by the third day the fighting ceased—the NVA had pulled back and was disengaging. A victory was declared by the American troops and two days later they were packed up and leaving Loc Ninh and heading off to some other hot spot.

Now it was our turn. Team A-331's asses were going to be on the line. The problem was that the NVA troops, while bloodied, were not defeated. They had simply slipped away from direct contact but had not retreated entirely. They were still out there in the jungle and we were here in our camp and they were coming to get us.

It took about a week for them to regroup before they hit us. They came from the east, through the rubber plantation, overrunning the village of Loc Ninh, and then attacked us in the middle of the night with mortars, 122mm rockets, and a human wave attack. They did not get as far into the wire this time as they had in August, but they tried and were very determined. The mortar barrages during the day would again last around 10 or 15 minutes, as the enemy would walk the mortar rounds across the compound.

We had plenty of air support with Cobra gunships blasting targets of opportunity. Puff was also back and firing its miniguns, while B-52 strikes arrived and were a little too close for comfort. Additional personnel reinforced us with three or four Special Forces soldiers from the B and C-Teams, temporarily assigned to the camp. None of them were medics but any help was greatly appreciated by all of us on the Team; we were exhausted from the lack of sleep and the effects of being on high alert for days.

Once again regular American troops returned and were camped out at the end of the runway. As before, the first night was the worst as far as ground assaults on the camp. But with the American troops engaging the NVA—pushing them out of the village of Loc Ninh and forcing them to retreat through the rubber plantation and into the jungle—the attacks on our camp over the next few nights were not that threatening.

Yes, their intent was still to overrun us, but it did not seem like their hearts were in it. Throughout this whole attack, which lasted for five days, we did not lose a single person. We had a lot of minor wounds from all the incoming mortar rounds, but no KIA's.

Up to this point I had always been the junior medic at Camp Loc Ninh. The acting senior medic when I arrived in May, Doc', had gone home. The senior medic that Doc' had been covering for, Lee Martin, DEROS'd in July. After Lee left, another senior medic transferred in and then transferred out almost immediately, so for a week I was the only medic in the camp. Another was soon assigned to us. He came from an A-Team up by Khe Sanh in I Corps where they had been under siege by the NVA for a couple of months. He thought that the Army had taken pity on him and was sending him to a safe A-Team camp with not much enemy activity.

I told him, "Man, you got screwed. We are and have been the most active (for enemy contact) A-Team in the III Corps area since I got here."

He was a SGT E-5 just like me. As I was giving him a tour around the camp we discovered that I had been promoted to SGT E-5 a month before he had, and therefore I was senior in rank to him. So now I was the senior medic.

"Oh shit!" was my reaction.

This was not something that I had strived for; as a matter of fact it did not even enter my mind until then. As we were talking and laughing about my new status as senior medic on the A-Team, our friendly local NVA mortar guy decided to set off a barrage and started walking mortar rounds across the camp. The first round hit when we were standing and talking out in the open. The second one hit while we were running. Before the third one hit we had both dived into a drainage ditch and were lying in the mud face down with our hands over our heads.

The mortar shells continued exploding across the camp with another five rounds arriving before the firing stopped. I took a small shell fragment through the heel of my right boot but it did not break the skin of my foot at all. No one else in camp was hit. It was more harassment by mortar than an all-out attack, but those rounds were still very deadly.

As we got up, now covered in mud, I said to my new junior medic, "Welcome to Loc Ninh."

Fortunately for him, he was able to transfer out in a month to a quieter place in Vietnam.

The rooting out of bad guys from the vicinity of the camp turned out to be another operation that we were excluded from. Regular troops and a Special Forces MIKE Force (Mobile Strike Force Command) combined to drive the NVA out of the village of Loc Ninh and push them back to Cambodia. Victory was declared and once more everyone pulled out and we were alone again and free to drive up and down our airstrip anytime we wanted.

SOG (Studies and Observation Group) was also involved in operations in our AO and used our camp as a staging area and launch site for their top-secret missions which often took them into Cambodia. One member of SOG, Sergeant George Kennedy, a medic classmate of mine, was in our camp for an afternoon. George and I caught up on things and talked about where some of our medic classmates were stationed in Vietnam before he had to leave on a mission.

When Loc Ninh was overrun by the NVA, many of the residents took refuge in the Catholic church in the village. The church had a French priest who was the last French person in the area. The French, who were formerly in charge of the rubber plantation, including their doctor, had left long ago and abandoned their mansions. They even had an Olympic-size swimming pool in their compound that was now in disrepair.

After the village of Loc Ninh was cleared of the NVA and everything quieted down, the French priest from the church came to our camp to ask for assistance with the 100 or so refugees that he was sheltering. I had never seen him before and was only vaguely aware of his existence. The team sergeant, Top, came up to me and said, "I've got a job for you *Bac Si*, see what you can do to help the priest."

I tried to talk with the priest but he could not or would not speak English and I could not speak French. The priest was very proficient in Vietnamese, but I didn't know enough to converse with him so we used one of the interpreters to communicate. The only French word beside *"merci"* (thank you) I could get out of what they were saying was "disinfectant." Through the interpreter the priest had said that he needed food, medical supplies, and disinfectant for the refugees in the church. I concluded after listening to him speak Vietnamese to the interpreter that he understood English pretty well.

I gathered up some bags of rice and some field rations that we issued to the CIDs, and got some medical supplies along with bags of lime. I then loaded everything up in a three-quarter-ton truck and off the interpreter

Author at a Cambodian New Year's Party, September 28, 1968.

and I went—me driving, he providing directions. When I pulled up to the church, I could see why the priest needed the disinfectant. During the siege, the refugees had been using an outside wall of the church as their restroom facilities and it stunk like hell. We unloaded the supplies from the truck with the help of Vietnamese who were still taking shelter in the church. The priest reassured us that they would take care of disinfecting the area and distributing the supplies. He thanked us for helping them out but I did not get a warm, fuzzy feeling from him. I don't think that he liked the American presence in Vietnam, and having to ask us for help must have really grinded at him.

The actions of the priest seemed suspicious to me. He could travel throughout the countryside and the VC did not bother him. We all wondered what kind of a deal he had made with them and whose side he was actually on. My mother had a cousin from Czechoslovakia who was a Catholic priest and had been in Burma during World War II, and was stationed in Hong Kong during the Vietnam War. He was not allowed to go home to Czechoslovakia because the Communists controlled that country and would not allow him back. I know from his letters to my mother that he hated the Communists. I didn't know if the French priest just did what he had to in order to survive or if maybe he was one of them.

I did meet the priest once more on my tour when an American unit was camped at the end of our airstrip. An American Catholic chaplain, who was attached to the unit, came into camp and wanted to have someone take him into the village to the Catholic church. The American chaplain had known the French priest when he was stationed in France during and immediately after World War II.

I was "volunteered" to drive the chaplain into Loc Ninh to meet with the priest. All was quiet in the area at that time so I wasn't too concerned for our safety, but still, I grabbed my M-16 and a claymore bag full of extra magazines. One can never be too careful. The chaplain, who I now noticed was a colonel, and I hopped into a jeep and drove down the side of the airstrip into Loc Ninh to the church.

The colonel/chaplain and the French priest met, embraced, and proceeded to talk in French so I had no idea what they were saying. The three of us went into the parsonage and sat at a table where drinks were served. It was a *liqueur* poured into a glass with some water added. It tasted like licorice. It was the first time I had ever had *liqueur*, especially French *liqueur*. The two of them conversed for a couple of hours, all in French, while I sat there. I wasn't bored. I was drinking some really potent stuff with a couple of Catholic priests and after a while I did not care anymore. I repeat, that stuff was potent!

Finally, it was time to go and I believe that all three of us were pretty tipsy, at least I was. The French priest was acting like we were the best of friends and he was hugging me as we left. I still figured that he was probably in bed with the VC in order to survive. But he wasn't a bad guy.

After I dropped the chaplain off at his unit and got back to camp, Top asked, "How was it?"

"Well it was quite boring to have to sit there with a couple of priests," I said.

But I was hoping that if the Catholic chaplain came back again I would get to drive him to the village and drink more of that French *liqueur*.

Around this time we received some very disturbing intelligence from some captured NVA documents. The documents included a complete layout of our camp detailed down to which rooms the American team members slept in. We knew that some of the CIDs had VC sympathies but none of them had access to the inner compound and surely would not know about our sleeping arrangements. So the regular CIDs were ruled out. This had to be an inside spying job.

To support the camp and the Civilian Irregular Defense Group personnel that we trained, housed, equipped, and fought alongside of, local villagers were hired to perform various essential jobs. These included a cook, two kitchen helpers, a cleaning crew, a carpenter, an electrician, a mechanic for the generators, and approximately five interpreters. The intelligence leak had to have come from one of them, as they were the only ones with total access to the inner compound.

The Army sent out a polygraph team along with their South Vietnamese counterparts to run lie detector tests on these employees. All but one passed. Our friendly Vietnamese electrician who always joked around with us and seemed to be an all-around good guy failed the polygraph test 100%. He kept declaring that he was not VC but the South Vietnamese took him away anyway. We later learned that under "further" interrogation he did finally admit that he was VC and had supplied all of the detailed camp layouts to the bad guys. None of us had ever suspected him. We never did hear what happened to him or anything more about him.

CHAPTER 9

AN EXECUTION

T HE OBJECTIVE OF AN upcoming five-day mission was to recon the area east of Village 10 and north of Highway 14. We had numerous intelligence reports that the NVA was infiltrating from Cambodia into this area and then heading south toward Saigon. Our job was to try to intercept the infiltrators and determine what their units were.

The NVA would travel in small groups of 10 to 12, usually led by a local VC sympathizer. The group would walk all day and spend the night in pre-dug bunkers in the ground that were covered over by logs. The next day they would move on to the next overnight bunker complex and continue moving from complex to complex as they infiltrated to the south. A second group would be right behind them, occupying the same bunkers where the first group had spent the previous night. Behind the second group would be a third group, and so on. With a new group heading out each day, the NVA could move a great deal of manpower undetected to their target in a short period of time. This is also how they transported supplies and ammo to the troops who had already infiltrated.

The rubber plantation ended at Village 10 and extended only a few klicks north of Highway 14. North of the plantation and east of the village was rain forest with semi-tall trees and thick underbrush. Cambodia was only four miles away. Our operation had made it up to Highway 14 and was walking in formation next to the highway on the south side in the rubber trees headed east. I say highway—it was a paved road but had not been used in years.

It did not look like any plantation workers had been removing the sap from the rubber trees in this area. The trees were not tapped and the little clay bowls that the sap was gathered in were nowhere to be seen. There were also weeds about four or five feet tall growing between the rubber trees, which were okay to walk through except some were covered with red ants. It stung like hell when they bit you. Even though the temperature was 90 degrees and the humidity was 90 percent, I kept my sleeves rolled down and my pants bloused into my boots to keep the ants from biting.

While walking along parallel to the road we came across an old punji stick field. The punji sticks were sharpened pieces of bamboo nearly one foot in length stuck in the ground at a 45-degree angle pointing toward the highway. There was a punji stick in every square foot of the field that was 20 feet wide and ran parallel to the highway for 100 feet or so. It appeared that the Viet Minh had once set up an ambush for the French on the opposite side of the road, hoping to drive the French into the punji sticks. All of the sticks were rotted and maybe half were broken off. This was the first time that I had ever seen a punji stick field and I guess I was not alone.

Buddhist temple near the CIDG family housing camp.

One of the older CIDs was explaining to some of the younger ones that, "The Viet Minh used punji stake fields like this for ambushes." I knew from my training that the VC had used this same tactic. The CID then said, "Now the VC have AK-47's so they don't need to use punji sticks no more."

Before we got to Village 10 we crossed the highway and made our way north through the rubber plantation for approximately two klicks. Once we were in the bushy jungle we then turned east. We did not want anyone to see us or to know which way we were going, since Village 10 was a known VC village. We stopped for the night and the next morning we continued moving east without seeing any signs of the enemy—no bunker complexes or anything else to indicate his presence. But the CIDs were becoming unusually quiet which meant they were uneasy and sensed there were bad guys in the area. The territory was all new to me, and I doubted that any of our patrols had been up this way for quite a while.

All of a sudden everyone stopped and dropped down to the ground and pointed their weapons to the north. I also got down and pointed my M-16 to the north. I could not see or hear anything.

A whisper quickly passed among the CIDs—"VC, VC, VC . . ."

I still could not see or hear anything, but one of the troops must have. Our formation was now stretched out close to 100 yards with all of us lying on the north side of a little path, including myself, with about four feet between each person. It was completely quiet for another two minutes with everyone down and their weapons ready and pointed to the north. I could barely detect the movement in the bush 30 yards in front of us, coming at an angle in our direction. Because of the dense underbrush, it wasn't until they were 25 yards in front of us that we could definitely identify them as VC.

All at once everyone opened up, including me. I fired off three 20-round magazines into which I had only loaded 19 rounds each (I had heard rumors that sometimes with 20 rounds the spring in the magazine became weak and would malfunction). I was spraying the area in front of me where I had seen shapes moving. The CIDs were blasting everything in front of them. Then, as quickly as it started, the firing stopped.

The CIDs were all yelling and some on either side of me rushed forward about 20 yards toward where the movement had been. I got up and stood there for a moment looking up and down the formation. It appeared that everyone was okay. The group of CIDs that had rushed forward were all yelling and pointing their weapons to the ground in front of them.

A couple of other CIDs ran over to where they were and called back at me, "VC, *Bac Si*, VC!"

I walked up to see what was going on with all the yelling and what I guessed to be cursing in Vietnamese. As I was moving forward I could see that the CIDs were standing over a wounded NVA soldier. As I got nearer I saw one of them pull down the pants of the wounded soldier and put his weapon into the groin area. I then noticed that the NVA was a young female. She was still alive with blood flowing from a couple of wounds. I was only 10 feet away, but before I could get there and do anything the CID put the tip of the barrel of his rifle up her vagina and fired three rounds.

I was stunned. I couldn't believe what had happened. Yes, she was certainly an NVA soldier and her AK-47, heavy with gun grease, was lying next to her. He had executed her. Just like that without any compassion. He had shot her up her vagina while she was lying completely defenseless on the ground. I guessed they were just pissed off because a *cô gái* (female) had fired at them.

I remained standing there in shock and could not fathom the situation. I watched the CIDs go through her backpack and pockets, taking all of her possessions. One of them reached down and took off a thin gold necklace she was wearing. There was a lot of talking and yelling going on between the CIDs standing over her now lifeless body. The one with the necklace came over to me and put it in my hand. A couple of the others said, "*Bac Si—caca dau!*" meaning that they thought I had killed her. Well, I might have hit her while firing my M-16 and knocked her down, but I sure did not kill her. She was still pumping blood when I had approached her.

As I stood there holding the necklace I knew this was an incident that I would never be able to get out of my mind.

We had run into a small group of NVA infiltrating into South Vietnam from Cambodia. We killed one and the others ran off. It did not stop the flow of troop movement heading south but maybe the identification that we obtained from the dead young female soldier would give the intelligence people a better picture of what was happening and where the NVA were going.

The rest of the operation was uneventful. We checked out Village 10 and then headed back to camp.

I kept that little gold necklace and brought it back home to the States with me but at some point I either lost it or threw it away.

CHAPTER **10**

OPERATIONS IN THE RUBBER

C AMP LOC NINH WAS in the middle of an old but still active French
rubber plantation. Many years ago, before a synthetic method of manufacturing was developed, the jungle had been cleared and planted with
rubber trees from which sap was extracted and then processed to make
rubber for tires. The trees were 50 to 60 feet tall and stood roughly 15 feet

*XO Lieutenant Sam Stokley (L) and author (R), prepared for
a mission, standing in front of main entrance to quarters.*

apart in rows that were 15 to 20 feet apart. In some places, in the middle of the rows, ditches four to five feet deep had been dug for what I assumed to be drainage, so the trees would be not be swallowed up by the swamp.

Walking through the rubber you could see rows going on and on in what seemed like an endless procession, as far as the eye could see. The lines of sight were excellent in every direction. It was a great place to patrol using what we called the "Roman box formation," with a fifth of the troops up front on point, a fifth on the right flank, a fifth on the left flank, a fifth in the rear, and a fifth in the center headquarters unit. If you got hit on any side, you could in theory reinforce that side and use one of the other elements to flank the bad guys. Moving through the rubber plantation in this fashion brought to mind what fighting in WWII Europe must have been like. No dense jungle to creep through, ample room for maneuvers, the ability to move about in a formation and see what was around you. It was way too cool.

I had very little idea of what the intelligence was at any given time regarding North Vietnamese Army movements, or what units were operating in our vicinity. I was a medic and I performed medical duties in camp, and was sent out with another team member on operations in the field. All I knew was that the night before a mission we would be given mission objectives in the Intelligence Room. We were shown on the big map where we were supposed to go and check things out. We would then mark our objectives on the personal map of the AO that we carried with us. We would confirm the codes for reporting our locations to the camp and then the next morning we would march out with the troops and be on our way.

On one particular mission we were patrolling in the rubber to the north of the camp because of reports of NVA infiltration through the area moving south. We were in Village 5, which was to the north of the camp on Highway 13, when we got word that the 11th Cav was assembled at the end of the runway at Loc Ninh, wanting to scout out this same area. It was decided that we would hook up and go on a joint mission with them. The CIDs were really excited. They loved the American GI's, myself and the other American team members excepted, as the GI's always kidded and joked with them whenever they were around.

The 11th Cav drove north up Highway 13 and arrived in no time at all. It was a lot faster than walking, our mode of transport, and they linked up with us in Village 5. Their force consisted of 10 armored personnel carriers. We coordinated with them and set off into the rubber, heading in a westerly direction. The CIDs were about 20 to 30 yards in front of the APC's and flanking them on all sides. This way, if we made contact, the CIDs and I could keep any RPG fire off the APC's, and we'd have the bad guys pinned down and engaged with us. Meanwhile the APC's, with their machine guns, would move up and clean them out. Once again, I kept thinking that this was like an American Army operation in WWII, except that our foot soldiers were Vietnamese, Montagnard and Cambodian. It was a great place for an armored operation, especially since the armor was ours and the enemy did not have any on this side of the Cambodian border.

As on most operations, things can get pretty boring—walking, looking out for bad guys, walking, resting, eating, walking, and then some more walking. Even with the APC's rolling along behind us, the novelty wore off quickly until without warning, we started receiving AK-47 fire from directly in front of us. I got behind a rubber tree and was firing in the direction from which we were being fired upon, and the CIDs were all behind rubber trees doing the same. We were taking gunfire but no RPG rockets. Normally, if you ran into an NVA unit they had at least one RPG per squad and would hit you with B-40 rockets, but this time there were no explosions. While we were shooting back, the APC's moved up to our line and unloaded with their machine guns. They tore up everything in front of us.

A couple of the 11th Cav guys were on top of the APC's, firing off M-79 grenade launchers. While the machine guns were roaring, the grenade launchers would go "bloop" when they were fired, followed by a loud "boom" ahead of us as the grenades exploded on the enemy's position; meanwhile the CIDs kept blasting away on full-automatic. The CIDs must have realized that the bad guys were pulling out and started to press forward. Some were running from tree to tree and using them for cover, while others advanced John Wayne-style and shot from the hip. We called these guys "Cowboys." During all of this, one of the 11th Cav guys fired his M-79, but to maximize its range he had it pointed on such a high elevation that the grenade blew up in a tree right in front of me. Luckily nobody was wounded but that was close; someone could have been taken out by friendly fire. The CIDs did that sort of thing all the time—maximizing the elevation on the M-79 and not accounting for a tree directly in front of them in the arcing path that the grenade would take. I guess it was just part of the learning curve in using an M-79.

We moved forward on line with the APC's and swept the area where the enemy had been firing from, but did not find any bodies, only a couple of blood trails. The NVA were always very good about recovering their dead and wounded. We continued to pursue them through the rubber which meant walking, resting, sweating, and walking some more. It seemed like the NVA had definitely *didi mau'd* (split) from the area. They didn't mind tangling with the CIDs but I figured they wanted no part of the 11th Cav, as they had nothing to match the firing capabilities of the APC's.

Our joint operation had gone very well. With the CIDs out front we had held off their rocket fire and kept the bad guys pinned down, unable to get off a good shot with their RPGs. And when we were engaged in the firefight with the NVA, the APC's with their heavy machine gun fire cut to shreds anything moving. We returned to Village 5 then hopped up on the back of the APC's and the 11th Cav gave us a ride down the highway back to camp. As we passed through the village of Loc Ninh, the CIDS were on top of the APC's acting like conquering heroes. I sure hoped that they would not steal too much stuff off them.

On another occasion while on an operation in the rubber north of the camp and west of Village 5, we were walking westerly through the plantation when suddenly all of the CIDs stopped and took cover behind the rubber trees. The right flank of the formation was now facing north. Apparently the CIDs had heard something or saw someone moving. Everything was quiet and I decided to see what was happening, and moved from one rubber tree to the next until I was one rubber tree behind where the CIDs were hunkered down.

I was down on one knee behind a rubber tree when I saw him—an NVA soldier approximately 50 yards down the row of rubber trees walking toward us. I remember thinking that he looked like Pancho Villa dressed in tan fatigues with crossed bandoliers of ammunition on his chest. I spotted him just as the CIDs opened fire toward the north.

I had Pancho Villa right in my sights and my M-16 set on semi-automatic. I had a clear shot. I squeezed off a few rounds and was sure that I hit him with the first one, but it seemed like he was still moving forward. Then I realized that when he was hit, the round had actually knocked him back a few feet. He was pushed back but remained in the standing position. This was a whole lot better than one time when I was carrying an M-2 carbine. I shot a bad guy with it but he kept coming forward. The carbine did not have the stopping power of an M-16.

I lost sight of Pancho Villa. He must have gone down. Since I no longer had a target I put the M-16 on full-auto and began to blast everything in front of me. It looked like we had, by luck, ambushed a squad of NVA moving through the rubber. The firing finally subsided and the CIDs began to pop out from behind the rubber trees and move carefully forward. Apparently, the bad guys had taken off.

Some of the CIDs near me pointed at the rubber tree I was crouching behind and were laughing. I stood up to see what they were laughing at. About four feet above my head, the tree bark was shot away and the milky white rubber sap was dripping all over the ground. My camo hat and my shoulders were covered by globs of the white sticky stuff. I knew that Pancho Villa didn't do that, so some of his buddies must have targeted me, though I hadn't seen them. When I was down behind the rubber tree firing ahead I had heard all kinds of loud cracking and snapping sounds. It was the sound of AK-47 rounds passing overhead and striking the rubber tree, missing my head by a matter of inches.

The CIDs moved forward and scouted the area where the bad guys had been but they didn't find any bodies. The NVA had carried them away. Seeing all that sap dripping down reinforced in my mind the correctness of my decision to fire at Pancho Villa on semi-automatic. I figured the bad guys must have been shooting at me on full-automatic, which meant the recoil from their rifles caused the bullets to go slightly to the right and upward, thus missing the intended target—namely me.

Shooting on semi-automatic one round at a time is the most effective way to hit a target. Lucky for me the bad guys hadn't done that, so I lived to tell the story of my encounter with Pancho Villa.

On another operation, SFC Andee Chapman and I were running a small recon patrol of 30 CIDs. We wove around Village 5 while heading north through the rubber plantation before proceeding west to its northern boundary. We then turned south toward camp while still on the lookout for any NVA activity.

The rubber plantation at the northern fringe was hilly and very scenic; the rubber tree rows meandered up and over the hills and stretched on for what seemed forever. There was no brush between the tree rows. The area had obviously been well tended to, and as we walked we could see everything between the rows of trees and beyond, unless the view was blocked by another hill. We were walking up a hill that was part of a chain of hills that ran east to west, with each one rising to about 40 to 50 feet in elevation and a good 200 yards between them. We had neared the top when the CIDs went down behind the trees and started pointing to the west while saying in whispered voices, "*Beaucoup* VC, *beaucoup* VC."

Andee and I got down behind some rubber trees and were looking to the west to see what was going on. I heard faint chopping sounds from the next big hill in front of us, and assumed the NVA were chopping logs to build bunkers. Usually they built their bunkers in the jungle, but this time must have decided to build them in the rubber plantation. The trees were so tall and leafy that it would be impossible to detect the bunkers from the air, and if they were on the north side of a hill they would be better protected from the US artillery fire from An Loc. Besides, the US or Vietnamese forces, and even our 105's in camp, were not allowed to fire into the rubber plantation unless we were in direct contact with the enemy. As the South Vietnamese government was trying to protect the old French colonial plantations, it was a very good place for Charlie to dig in.

We carefully moved up to the top of the hill to get a better look at what was going on. Looking down the rows of rubber trees I could not see a thing. Nothing. No movement at all. Although the bad guys were out of our sight, we could very distinctly hear the chopping sounds coming from the northwest side of the next hill. After listening awhile we decided that it was not in our best interest to move toward the chopping activity. There were probably guards posted everywhere and we didn't have a clue as to how many enemy soldiers we might encounter.

Yeah, we could move in and surprise them but we had only 30 guys. Based on all the chopping sounds, they could be a company-size unit of

roughly 100 to 150. After the initial surprise assault we would have probably been toast. So talking in whispers, we radioed the camp to request
some artillery support and were able to get the 175mm American guns at
An Loc for a fire mission.

A big 175 fired a locating shot which Andee adjusted, and then two
more shots followed which he adjusted further to be closer to the site of
the chopping sounds. The fourth round was right on target and Andee
gave them the okay to "fire for effect"—meaning to just start blasting at
the previous coordinates. Every 20 seconds a shell would hit and explode
on the back side of the next hill.

As the shells were exploding, I spotted an enemy soldier behind a rubber tree looking our way. He was 20 or 30 yards from the base of the next
hill. The NVA must have told their lookouts to try to determine where the
artillery was being called in from. At first, the lookout was hugging a rubber
tree about 150 yards away while peeking around to see if he could detect
anything. Though he was looking in our direction, he probably could not
spot us. The only thing in his line of sight was whatever was between the
rubber trees in the row he was in, and I was low down on the ground and
behind a rubber tree.

The CIDs on either side of me were also down on the ground hiding
behind the trees. The NVA lookout kept peeking around as shells were
falling behind him. He must have gained confidence that there was nothing
in our direction, because he slowly moved into the middle of the row, then
haltingly walked toward us while trying to get a better view. He still could
not see me or the other CIDs. I could distinctly see him with his weapon
in front of him, holding it in the port position with both hands. I continued watching while being careful not to move or make a sound when
"BOOM"—the spot where he was standing erupted in a giant explosion.
I kept watching to see what had happened, but once the smoke and dust
cleared there was not a trace of him. I mentally marked the spot where he
had been.

After five minutes we called off the artillery and told them we would
give them a sit-rep (situation report), but to stay zeroed in on the target
while we assessed the damage. Although the chopping sounds disappeared,
and we could not hear any other activity, we wanted those 175mm guns
to be ready to provide fire support in case we ran into a large force of NVA.

As we moved out I kept the location of the bad guy in the middle of the rubber tree row in my head.

We proceeded carefully toward the hill, going from one rubber tree to the next. As we approached the location of the spotter, who I'm sure had been hit, there was no sign of him. I looked all around where he had been and where the shell had exploded, but there was nothing. The shell had landed right on top of him and must have simply evaporated him. After a brief recon of the hillside where the chopping sounds had come from, we did not locate any bodies, only the remnants of some logs. The bad guys had all bugged out. They must have retreated into the jungle further to the west during the artillery barrage.

There was nothing more we could do here so we continued on south toward camp. We did give the big guns a body count of three. I was certain of one and we figured that we probably got a couple more. It was just good PR to give the artillery guys a body count so that the next time you needed them, they would be more likely to fire knowing that they were doing some good for you and damage to the bad guys. But as for the NVA soldier in the middle of the rubber row, he had vanished.

CHAPTER 11

ADVENTURES AT VILLAGE 2

VILLAGE 2 WAS A Viet Cong village. The South Vietnamese government had no control over it, and we were the only guys on our side that ever went there. The villagers were sympathizers who supported and assisted the local VC and their allies, the NVA troops that moved through the area. They also supplied manpower—husbands and sons—to the VC cause. Any time I was there I noticed there were only women and children; the men and older boys were always gone. And each time we operated a patrol to the east of the camp near Village 2, we seemed to have some type of contact with the bad guys.

To get to Village 2, we had to leave camp and head northeast alongside the airstrip runway, proceed a half-mile toward the village of Loc Ninh, then turn right and walk four miles through the rubber plantation toward the jungle. Village 2 was right at the edge of the jungle. It did not take long to get there, as four miles through the rubber was a very easy walk. No brush, no big hills, no streams or other obstacles. Just row upon row of rubber trees.

There was a small one-lane gravel road from Loc Ninh to Village 2 that was traversable by car. The French priest at the Catholic church in Loc Ninh had a Citron that he would drive to the village as part of his rounds; somehow he was able to travel the countryside unimpeded by the VC. If we were going straight to Village 2 we would follow that road, which was the main drag of each village. The only problem with this was that we were sure there were local spies in Loch Ninh who would take off ahead of us and let the people in Village 2 know we were coming, so they could alert the local VC.

One time when we were in the rubber plantation heading for Village 2, we heard some kind of clanking sounds in front of us. The women who were working there were banging together the small clay dishes they used to collect the sap from the trees, and this was making the clanking noise. They were alerting the local VC in Village 2 that we were coming. We saw them scurrying ahead of us, then banging their bowls together, but we couldn't or wouldn't shoot them. They were unarmed, and even though they were letting the bad guys know that we were on the way, they did not present any immediate danger to us. They were probably warning their VC husbands and sons or other male relatives. Besides, they were mostly old toothless women.

When we arrived at Village 2 there were only some very old men, women, and small children there. The men and young boys must have slipped away into the jungle. Still, we always treated the villagers kindly, never harassing them or ransacking their huts. We would talk to some of them but it was always the same story, "No VC here." It was simply a fact: they were all Viet Cong and on the other side in this conflict. The CIDs searched all of the hidden bomb shelters and the only thing they found was a baby mouse in one of them. They brought the baby mouse to me and said "VC *Bac Si*, VC." I laughed with them and grabbed my radio and pretended to call back to camp, "*Mot* (one) VC captured." Then we all laughed as they let the little baby mouse go, saying to him "*Di* (go) VC, *di*."

Another time we came into the village from the south side, hoping to catch some local VC or uncover arms caches they might have hidden there. We swept the village without allowing anyone to run off and began to search each hut in the village. We did not find any VC or any hidden arms or ammunition. One thing we did discover was that almost every single hut had a small hole hidden in the floor that was like a bomb shelter, capable of holding two or three people. Neither we, nor the South Vietnamese, had ever shelled or mortared the village but it looked like the villagers were ready for it.

On one five-day, multi-company operation, on our second day out, we approached the village from the jungle side. On this side there was a large hill where you could see quite a ways in each direction. At the top of the hill we encountered a young boy about 10 years old. The troops sneaked up on him as he was playing and not paying attention to what was going on around him. He was a spotter for the VC and was up on the hill to alert the others if he saw any troop movements. He was only 10 years old, but definitely VC.

The CIDs were rough on him and he was scared shitless. I wondered now what should we do with him? Some of the CIDs were threatening to shoot him but I wouldn't let them, though we couldn't just let him go and run home and tell the bad guys our position and strength. We would always rather find the VC than have the VC find us. The outcome would likely be more favorable for our side if we were not ambushed by theirs.

The young boy said, "Don't know where VC is," and kept maintaining his innocence. Just the same, his job was to watch for any troop movements and report back to the village. Being a 10-year-old, it must have been a very boring and lonely job sitting up on the hilltop all day, and he had screwed up. The only reasonable thing to do was to take him along with us on the rest of our operation. I kept him close to me for the next three days and three nights and shared my rations with him. I always carried a bag of rice with me that I knew was more than I would eat during the whole five days, so I cooked up a canteen cup of it for him for every meal. Along with the rice, I shared some of my C-rations with him. The boy seemed to enjoy the food. He also calmed down, and by the second day had gotten over his nervousness with us, as he was being fed and well treated. He no longer seemed to fear for his safety and must have believed he was on some really wild adventure.

Fortunately, or unfortunately, we never did run into any bad guys on that patrol. On the fifth day, while on our way back toward the village of Loc Ninh and the camp, we let him go. He scurried off to Village 2. I'm sure he had a very interesting story to tell. The only other option was to bring him back to camp and turn him over to the South Vietnamese Army. All they would do is torture him and throw him into some kind of prison where they would torture him some more and starve him half to death.

Christ, he's only 10 years old, I thought. So off the boy went to tell his story.

———————

As I say, it seemed like every time we approached good old Village 2, we got into some kind of action. On another five-day operation we had stopped right at the edge of the rubber, a couple klicks south of the village, to take a break before going into the thick jungle. Everyone was sitting down, making some rice for their meal and taking a rest, when we began to get hit by mortar rounds. They were from a 61mm mortar and were landing all around us, exploding in the rubber trees and on the ground. I could hear the rounds being fired due south of us. The enemy most likely had the weapon set up in a little clearing that existed between the rubber plantation and the jungle.

The CIDs were all scurrying about trying to find safety by lying in depressions in the ground or hiding behind the rubber trees. The incoming fire was very accurate so there must have been someone close enough to see us and to direct it. If we stayed and hid behind the trees I knew the mortar would chop us up and blow us to pieces. We had to do something and quick.

I yelled at the CIDs, *"Di--di"!* (run) and took off in the direction of the mortar firing sounds. A few of the CIDs nearest me began running with me. Then the rest of the CIDs all jumped up and were running with us. It was our only chance of escaping the mortar fire. We were now just a mob running through the rubber trees. We could still hear the mortar being fired ahead of us, but the rounds were all falling behind us. A mortar has a distinct sound when a round is fired—a loud "poof." We charged and kept running toward the "poof" sounds. That was our only way out. About 50 yards into the run we saw a couple of NVA in tan uniforms moving away from us. They fired in our direction and we returned fire. It was no match. There were two of them and we had some 25 CIDs up front blasting away. I stopped and had one of the NVA in my sights and got off a magazine or so. One of the CIDs was slightly off to my left and 10 feet in front of me. He was hiding behind a rubber tree and did not even attempt to see the bad guys or to shoot.

Things subsided as the NVA soldiers were no longer in view or shooting at us, and the mortar fire had ceased. We had outrun the mortar attack and chased the bad guys off. The little CID who was hiding behind the tree to my left then started to holler at me, *"Bac Si* shoot past me; I afraid that *Bac Si* shoot me."

I yelled back at him, "If you weren't hiding behind that tree you could have shot at the VC and I wouldn't have had to."

The whole time we kept advancing toward the mortar fire, though now in a much more orderly fashion, as we were no longer running. At some point during our rush forward they must have seen us coming and taken off. After proceeding 50 yards or so we found one dead NVA who had been shot two or three times and was lying face down. The CIDs searched the area but did not find any others. They had taken off through the jungle with their little mortar, but we got one of them for sure. A couple of the CIDs had sustained some minor surface shrapnel wounds resulting from the mortar fire, but no one was seriously injured.

We rolled the dead enemy soldier over onto his back and the CIDs started to go through his pockets and loot whatever they could find. Based on his uniform and insignia, he was definitely NVA, and not a local. In his wallet they found a picture of a beautiful young Vietnamese woman and showed it to me. She was wearing one of the typical conical straw hats and dressed in what we called "black silk pajamas." She was probably his girlfriend or wife. After I looked at the photo, I took it from the CID and placed it back in the dead soldier's front shirt pocket. She would never see

Sgt Tom Reisinger (left), author (center), plus unidentified soldier, before leaving for an operation.

him again. We placed a *Chieu Hoi* (open arms surrender) poster on his chest. These posters offered any VC or NVA who surrendered to us 50 dollars for their weapon, almost a month and a half's wages, with no questions asked.

The CIDs were so pissed about being mortared that they rolled the NVA's body over and put a grenade under him with the pin pulled so that if anyone were to move him or try to pick him up, the grenade would explode. A dirty trick and probably against the laws of warfare, but the bad guys would do the same. Where we were, there were no laws or rules of warfare, it was kill or be killed. The enemy had taken off into the thick jungle and was long gone. Since it was part of our mission objective to patrol to the south of Village 2, we set off after them.

The jungle at the edge of the rubber plantation was dense with branches, vines, weeds, short and tall trees. It was very slow going because we had to chop and hack our way along. Once again the CIDs up front would create a small pathway that was just big enough for them, which meant I had to duck down to make it through. Doing this, while carrying a backpack with provisions for five days and toting ammo and an M-16, made for hard and exhausting travel.

On the third day we reached our first objective to the south and east of Village 2, where the jungle gave way to bamboo thickets. The bamboo grew in dense clusters some three or four feet in diameter that was impossible to penetrate. The only thing you could do was walk and weave your way between the clusters that seemed to be everywhere.

When I attempted to string up my sleeping hammock that night I tied it between the two biggest bamboo shoots I could find. But once I climbed into the hammock, the bamboo would bend over and, as happened previously, I wound up lying on the ground. The CIDs didn't have that problem, as they were a whole lot lighter. They chuckled at me in my big saggy hammock.

"*Bac Si* too *beaucoup*," they said.

On the fourth day we checked out the last objective of our recon in the jungle. We had not found any signs of the bad guys or the NVA that had mortared us earlier. We were heading back to camp, a good day-and-a-half walk, when all kinds of gunfire broke out. I didn't know if we had jumped the bad guys or had found their base camp, but the two sides having just met up were exchanging a hail of bullets. With all of the bamboo thickets around, you could not see more than 10 feet in any direction. It was difficult to tell what was going on.

I slowly moved up to where the gunfire was coming from, being careful as I wormed between each cluster of bamboo. I was getting closer to the action and crouching down on one knee, then hit the dirt when the tall thicket in front of me was cut down by half, to about head high, from enemy machine gun fire. The thicket, which had been some four feet in diameter and 12 feet tall, was still four feet in diameter but now only six feet tall. While lying flat on the ground, I made a mental note of the fact that "bamboo won't stop shit," and tried to see where the firing had come from. I did not shoot back as I could not tell where the bad guys were, or where our CIDs were. I had an equally good chance of hitting a friendly up front as I did an enemy.

Then all at once it was over. The firing stopped. We regrouped to determine what had happened. The best we could figure is that we had encountered a squad of NVA coming through the bamboo. None of our guys were hit and we did not know if we had hit any of them. I guessed that neither side could tell what they were shooting at and had simply blasted away at everything in front of them. The NVA must have thought that there were a whole lot more of us than there were of them, and took off to save themselves.

That's what our CIDs would often do as well. If there were more of the bad guys than there were of us, or even if the sides looked even, they would *didi mau* and get the hell out of there. So these bad guys weren't so much different.

We made our way back to camp arriving in the village of Loc Ninh around noon on the fifth day. Loc Ninh was divided in two by a small river running through it. As it was formerly the headquarters for the old French rubber plantation, the buildings were constructed mostly of some type of masonry or mud brick, as opposed to the straw huts in the smaller villages. About 900 Vietnamese lived there, and no Cambodians or Montagnards. The village even had a small "downtown market place" with little open-air shops that sold everything from sandals to ducks and eels.

Along the bank of the river was a small restaurant/cafe where you could buy a semi-cold Coca Cola or a Vietnamese iced coffee made with very sweet milk or cream. Whenever we passed through Loc Ninh at the end of a mission, it was my custom to stop at the little restaurant and buy a Coke for my radio man and me. I'm sure that I paid twice as much as a Vietnamese would pay for the Cokes but after a five-day mission through the countryside, I didn't care.

———————

At another time I was on an operation with about 100 CIDs, and we were working our way back to camp from out in the jungle in the vicinity of Village 2. It was unusual in that we had been beating the bush for four days without encountering any bad guys. We were moving in formation in two columns roughly following an east-west trail. Then, maybe a klick from the edge of the rubber plantation, everyone got down and became real quiet. The wind was blowing from the west and one of the CIDs walking point said he smelled rice wine in the breeze. We maintained a tight formation while keeping on both sides of the trail and in the cover of the bush. The CIDs on point were carefully and quietly advancing while the rest of us moved up behind them.

All at once the CIDs on the left side of the trail began to open up on someone or something in front of them. When that happened, the CIDs on the right side of the trail opened up, but what they were shooting at I didn't know. It's a natural response that when someone starts to fire, you fire also, if only to protect yourself. Our left column received some AK-47 fire for a few moments and now all the CIDs were shooting and rushing forward on both sides of the trail. I slowly worked my way toward the front. I did not fire my own weapon as all of our guys were still ahead of me. But I could tell that whatever or whoever they were firing at had run off. When I arrived at the front, the CIDs were standing around on the left side of the trail.

The enemy had apparently set up an ambush for anyone coming from the west. There were only about three or four of them, and they must have gotten pretty bored staying in their ambush position for so long, so they started to drink rice wine. And for our troops to be able to smell it from a distance, it must have been a lot. The bad guys were set to ambush anyone headed east on the trail but we had approached them from their backside. We had snuck up on them and jumped their little ambush. I really don't know if any of them were hit. We didn't come across any bodies and it was almost impossible to find blood trails in the jungle. We also could not tell if they were local VC or regular NVA troops. I just figured that we must have caused at least couple of them to have to change their pants when they finally stopped running.

CHAPTER 12

THANKSGIVING DINNER

—————

T HE PATROL WAS A five-day, small company-size operation that we were due back from on Thanksgiving Day, 1968. I was told that there had been a ceasefire for Christmas and the Vietnamese New Year (*Tet*), but since the bad guys violated the ceasefire earlier this year, nobody trusted them anymore. In Vietnam, Thanksgiving was just another work day. Most of our indigenous troops had never heard of it, or if they had, they did not understand it. Neither side observed a ceasefire for Thanksgiving.

The Team Room dining facility at Loc Ninh; at left is SSgt Larry Taylor, sitting with unidentified man.

On television you often saw American troops having turkey with all the fixings and a big Thanksgiving Day bash. At the A-Team camp at Loc Ninh, we were on separate rations and I'm certain we did not have a turkey, much less a pumpkin pie. Since Thanksgiving was the fifth day of the patrol and I expected we would return to camp that afternoon, I didn't pack any rations for that day—nothing, nada. For a special treat on Wednesday, I had opened a can of turkey C-rations. I usually ate the biggest cans of C-rations on the first couple of days out and saved the smaller cans (turkey was among the smaller ones) for days three and four. It made for less weight in my backpack at the end of a mission. By day five I figured I did not have to carry anything, expecting to eat once I got back to the camp. I would only carry about half a bag of rice those days and would split it into four portions for the first four days.

Each CID got a whole bag of rice for each day of patrol. They could sure pack that rice away.

By noon on the fourth day out we had achieved our objective in the northeast part of the AO and found nothing. We were ready to head back to camp. We radioed in to the team, "The area is clear and we are going to start back."

The CO came on the radio and said, "You have new orders; your operation is extended for three more days." We were to proceed a little further north toward a "high-priority area" and secure a landing zone on the morning of the sixth day for a re-supply. I didn't see a reason to stay out for another three days. The whole area was quiet and deserted, but orders are orders. Someone, somewhere, must have had extra helicopters for the day that they wanted to use, or Intel really had received a report that there was NVA activity in the vicinity. The only way this affected me was that I did not have anything to eat for the day. The CIDs were a little low on food but could manage, because even on the fifth day out they were still cooking up big breakfasts and lunches of rice. I knew they would not starve.

That night we entertained ourselves by trying to pick up radio transmissions from the Special Forces Team at Bu Dop. Bu Dop was the next camp to the east of us, and though we could not normally raise them on our PRC-25 radios, we were near their AO. We didn't know what radio frequency they were using, but for a couple of hours kept trying to tune them in. My medic classmate, Julian Aguilar, was a medic on their team and I thought it would be cool to call him, but we never did find their radio frequency.

On the morning of the fifth day we came across a small abandoned hamlet in the jungle. It looked like it had been uninhibited for a long time, with only the buildings' foundations still in place. At the edge of the hamlet there was a small grove of about 20 banana trees. The bananas were three to four inches long and were kind of tough, but we all gorged ourselves on them. They were the first bananas that I had seen or eaten since being in Vietnam. I didn't even know they were grown here. The bananas were all I had to eat on that Thanksgiving Day.

After we feasted on the bananas we moved out for the night. On the morning of the sixth day we found an open area for an LZ and were re-supplied by helicopter. Our people back at camp must have had sympathy for us, because the re-supply included a sandbag full of cold beers. My teammate and I each had two cold ones and I gave a couple to our LLDB counterpart and one to each of our radio operators. The remainder of the beer was divided up among the troops. The rest of the patrol was uneventful as we checked out the "high-priority area" and found nothing.

We made it back to camp at noon on Sunday, the eighth day. As I suspected, there was no leftover turkey because there never was one.

CHAPTER 13

MEDICAL DUTIES IN CAMP

B ECAUSE WE WERE IN a combat zone we had to have on hand medications such as Demerol and morphine to relieve pain from severe
wounds. Both of these drugs are opiates and highly addictive and therefore
regulated in the USA, as they were on an A-Team in Vietnam. They remained in the small safe in the medical bunker at all times, along with a
general stock of medications for use in case of an attack on the camp when
it was not safe to be in the dispensary. The only time they were removed
was when used to treat a patient, in the case of Demerol, or allotted to a
team member to carry on a mission, in the case of morphine.

The senior medic kept a log accounting for the administration and

Nurses cleaning the medical storage cabinet in the medical bunker.

allocation of these two narcotics under the recipient's name. The net amount of the drugs in the safe had to match the beginning amount of the drug in the log, less the amounts administered or allotted. Army inspectors would pop in unannounced and demand to see the log sheets and would do an inventory of the narcotics on hand. This happened to me a couple of times and in each case my inventory was right on the dot, not too much and not too little. This was a result of good record keeping on my part, and knowing how to tweak the system.

As Demerol was only injected into a patient in a clinical situation, it was very easy to keep track of. Morphine was something else. Each team member going on patrol (two to a patrol) would be issued a couple of field dressings and five ampules of morphine each. The dressings were basically for themselves, as the CIDs had their own medics who carried enough for their own people. The morphine we carried on patrol was for use on anyone who was wounded that required it. We did not trust the CIDs with morphine, but the LLDB on the operation also carried some that was issued to him by the LLDB *Bac Si* who had his own supply.

On an operation when you are in contact the first priority is to defeat the enemy and to survive. When engaged in firefight things get confusing and can happen real fast and the least of your worries is keeping track of your five ampules of morphine. They get lost, left behind, or just misplaced

Two individuals in front of the entrance to the medical dispensary.

and are unaccounted for on the battlefield. When an operation returned to camp, one of my team members might say to me, "*Bac Si*, I lost my morphine and need some more of that shit."

I knew that no one was using morphine or on drugs and that they probably did really lose it. The problem was, losing morphine was not a justifiable entry into the log-book. Inspectors, who had probably never seen any type of combat whatsoever, would not accept it as a legitimate explanation. So if I was, say, five ampules short in the inventory I had to somehow make up for the loss. The way I would do this was to over-allocate it in the log-book to patients requiring an injection of morphine. I would never deny anyone any morphine if their wounds required it, nor would I fudge the amount of morphine used on a patient being medevac'd. But if one of our troops was KIA, I could and sometimes would indicate that he received two or three ampules of morphine instead of the one or none that he actually did receive. By doing this a few times, I was able to build up an additional supply. This surplus morphine I kept in a secret stash in the medical bunker for use the next time someone on an operation lost his. Thus, the narcotics log-book was always right on and my ass was covered for inspections.

I was the senior medic at Camp Loc Ninh from September 1968 to May 1969, after having been the junior medic on the team prior to that. My duties while in camp ranged from supervising morning sick calls and dealing with medical emergencies to overseeing basic sanitation practices. With between 500 to 700 CIDs, for whom I was their primary *Bac Si*, there were always at least 20 or 30 reporting to sick call every day in the dispensary. They would have ailments ranging from the common cold or minor shrapnel wounds that needed to be re-dressed, to tropical diseases such as ringworm or even malaria. Fortunately for me, my counterpart LLDB medic, *Bac Si* Cong, and the other CID medics, had been very well trained by the previous Special Forces medics stationed at Loc Ninh and could handle the everyday sick call situations.

The dispensary was a rectangular-shaped, wood-sided, above-ground building with a tin metal roof situated just inside the front gate of the camp. As you entered there was a small work station to screen persons reporting for sick call. To the right was an enclosed pharmacy that was kept locked when not manned by a CID pharmacist, which contained basic medications for treating most common conditions. It did not contain any narcotics. On the left side of the dispensary were four wooden beds for treating those with minor conditions. The beds were not used for overnight stays, as we were not prepared or equipped to take care of patients who were bedridden for any significant period of time. In addition, with its tin roof, we could not insure the safety of anyone in there during a mortar attack. The roof would do nothing to stop a mortar round and if a patient was in the dispensary and bedridden, they would be a sitting duck.

Past the pharmacy on the right side there were two small offices, one for *Bac Si* Cong and one for the Special Forces medics. The rear of the building was a large operating room with an operating table, supplies, and equipment for semi-major surgery. We tried to keep the operating room as sterile as possible and all of the instruments were autoclaved (sterilized) by the nurses. We did the best we could during an operation, wearing masks and gloves and using sterile instruments, but then a fly might come buzzing past your head. The best we could do under *these* conditions, anyway. Wounds to the head, chest, and abdomen, or wounds that would require overnight or longer stays, we medevac'd out—we were not trained or qualified to operate on these. The motto of a Special Forces medic was to "First Do No Harm."

The basic staffing for the dispensary included *Bac Si* Cong and a senior CID medic who had been trained at the C-Team hospital to treat colds, perform minor surgery, and debride wounds. There was a CID pharmacist who would dispense the prescribed medications and three nurses, one Vietnamese and two Cambodian. We had a second CID medic back at the C-Team hospital being trained for sick call duty and to perform minor surgery. During a typical sick call there was not much for me to do unless the CID medics encountered something they were not sure of. Using my notes from the Special Forces medical training classes and/or the Merck manual, I would then treat the patient the best I could.

———————

Malaria was one of the most common diseases in Vietnam. Those diagnosed with it could usually be treated during sick call with anti-malarial drugs and would respond to treatment. Every US Special Forces team

Sgt. Tom Reisinger, in front of the Civic Action Building, the Special Intelligence unit attached to Loc Ninh.

member was required to take one pill a week to ward off malaria. We were lucky because in some areas of Vietnam a more potent form was prevalent, which required taking a daily pill.

I soon learned that trying to get someone to take a pill when they had no immediate symptoms was very frustrating and difficult. In the team room there was a dry eraser board with each team member's name on it. To the right of their names was a calendar for them to initial when they had taken their weekly malaria pill. I was a real pest and pain in their ass about it. Captain, lieutenant, master sergeant—it didn't matter. Eventually they realized it was easier for them to take the pill than to have me on their ass until they did. They'd grumble but would finally take it.

The indigenous personnel in Vietnam, whether Vietnamese, Montagnard, or Cambodian, were not able to take the weekly pill. I was told they had a slightly different blood type that would cause them to have a reaction to it. Therefore, I could not prevent them from getting malaria. I could only treat them when they came down with it.

The only form of protection we could offer was to supply them with mosquito netting for their bunks. The mosquito netting when tucked into the mattress on a bunk also kept the rats from running over you at night. In addition, I tried to eliminate standing pools of water around the camp to prevent mosquitos from breeding.

———————

Being a medic on an A-Team meant that you are on-call all of the time. If there was a medical situation or an emergency, you responded. It didn't matter if it was in the middle of the night and you had to be awakened or if you'd drunk yourself into oblivion earlier that evening. Someone came and got you and you had to wake up or sober up real quick and respond to the situation. The main reason that I would get called in after hours was because someone had brought one of the CIDs to the dispensary. They would often be burning up with fever while having severe chills and shaking all over.

I'd first go into the team room and get a bag of ice cubes from one of the deep freezers, then walk down to the dispensary along with the person that had been sent to get me (usually one of the nurses or a CID medic). In the dispensary the patient would be lying on one of the wooden beds, shaking from head to foot. *Diagnosis step one: chills.*

I would approach the patient and feel his forehead and chest and they would be burning up with fever. No need to take a temperature, they were hot as hell. *Diagnosis step two: fever.*

I would then take a good look at the patient's eyes. Ninety-nine percent of the time they were severely jaundiced. The whites of their eyes would be yellowish in color and their skin in the facial and chest area would likewise be yellowish. *Diagnosis step three: jaundice.*

That was enough for me. No need to feel for an enlarged spleen or run complicated blood tests. The patient was diagnosed with a malaria attack and I would start treating the symptoms. First thing would be to place ice on the patient's forehead and chest to reduce the fever. Second thing was to administer anti-malarial medication and something else to further reduce the fever. The third thing, if the patient was severely dehydrated, was to get a normal saline IV started. And the last thing, once they came out of the fever and chills, was to get them to come into sick call the next morning for more treatment. They would probably do that in order to get additional medication, but as the effects of the malaria attack wore off they would think they were cured and would no longer take the medication. In that case, I could expect to see them again in the future in the middle of the night shivering, shaking, and burning up with fever.

That went for my American teammates as well. If they came down with something they would come directly to me and I would treat them. But quite often, if I prescribed some medication to take for 10 days, they would feel better after five or six days and stop taking it. In that respect they were no different from the CIDs. Any thoughts I may have had about entering the medical profession went right down the toilet; I got too upset from treating people and then seeing them not follow the regimen for the necessary period of time.

I considered what the average GP doctor treated, gallbladder problems for instance, for which the classic signs were the Four F's—female, forty, fat, and flatus. The fact that I probably wasn't smart enough to get into medical school also entered into the equation.

The biggest competitor I had for medical services was the "Chinese Medicine Man" (witch doctor), in Loc Ninh. We didn't compete in the treatment of battle wounds but we did with common colds, flu, fevers, etc. Though I never did meet him, nor did I understand what his regular course of treatment was, I often saw the signs of his work. All I did know was that if someone came in to see me and they were very sick, I could tell if they had first gone to him by the red suction cup marks on their neck and chest. He was their primary source for treatment, but once his "medicine" didn't work they would come to me and I would cure them with my modern methods.

One morning our Vietnamese CID nurse, who was a very good nurse, came into the dispensary with red suction cup marks on her neck. She had had a cold and gone to my competitor. I asked her about it and she sheepishly admitted that it was true—she had seen the Chinese Medicine Man. All I could do was shake my head at her.

———————

Though the average CID private got paid approximately $30 a month, I'm sure they did not get to keep it all since they had to pay their platoon sergeant a "monthly fee" (kickback). It was common knowledge that there was a system of bribes and corruption. The platoon sergeant then had to pay a fee to the person he reported to. This went right up the chain of command with the CID company commander getting his cut.

The CID privates would always have some of the money from their pay to burn. The local custom in Vietnam, whether you were Catholic or Buddhist, was that you could have as many wives as you were able to support, with each in a separate household. But the CID privates did not make enough to support a household.

There were no taboos on marriage or sex in Vietnam. Often the unmarried CIDs would go to the village of Loc Ninh with their leftover pay where they could drink and engage in other activities. On a back street there, a "Mama-san" ran a little whorehouse that usually had three young Vietnamese prostitutes working. It was a favorite stop for the young CIDs with a pocket full of money.

During a typical morning sick call the CIDs came in with all the normal illnesses and maladies. Then all of a sudden you would get one or two, and then the next day three or four, coming in with gonorrhea (the clap) that they had contracted from one of Mama-san's girls. I'd heard all the stories of penicillin-resistant strains of gonorrhea in Vietnam but fortunately we only had the good old normal clap in our area.

Now the choice was simple—to either keep treating more and more CIDs for the clap as the days went on, or to eliminate it at its source. I chose to visit the Mama-san and to treat the infection at the source, the infected girl. Most of the time, it was not that dangerous to hop into a jeep and drive into Loc Ninh during the daylight hours. The village was crawling with the RFPF troops from down the road guarding the village, and also some of our CIDs doing whatever in town.

So off I'd go in a jeep, with a small medical bag and an interpreter, to Mama-san's. I'm sure I would never have found it by myself, but the location of the whorehouse was common knowledge in the village.

The Mama-san was appreciative of the visit. If one of the CIDs got the clap they might come back and beat the crap out of the girl who had infected him. If the girl got all beat up, she would be out of action for a couple weeks or so and, as in any business, time is money. I would take the girl with gonorrhea back into her little room and inject her with a big dose of penicillin in the butt, plus give her some oral penicillin to take for

10 days. Next, I would assemble all of the girls and give each of them a bottle of antibacterial soap. I would tell them to wash their private parts right after sex and then to immediately urinate. I said that by doing this they could eliminate most of the clap.

After giving my little public health lecture through the interpreter, the girls would giggle and scoot off to their rooms. I'm really not sure if they listened to me, but once the "sick" girl (or girls), was treated, the incidence of gonorrhea cases at the dispensary would drop down to zero for a month or so. I would talk to the Mama-san and tell her that the "sick" girl would not be able to work for a week until she was cured. She would always thank me and offer me a drink of iced tea or a beer. Also, the services of a girl for free if I so desired. I always chose a beer in a bottle. The tea had ice in it made from the local water and I would not drink any water unless it was chlorinated or treated. As for the girl, I figured if one had the clap another one probably did too and I did not want to take that chance. As I did not understand much of Vietnamese, the interpreter might well have chosen the girl option for himself for a later time. To think, I was 24 years old and living the dream of a great deal of young men: I was working in a whore-house!

CHAPTER 14

MEDICAL MEDCAPS

ONE OF THE OBJECTIVES of an A-Team during the war in Vietnam was to "win the hearts and minds" of the Vietnamese people. Essentially, we were trying to get the general populace to like us and the South Vietnamese government more than they liked the Viet Cong and the North Vietnamese. The problem was that the South Vietnamese, other than having a government-appointed district chief in Loc Ninh, had little control or influence over the outlying hamlets. The hamlets were never visited by government officials or ARVN units, and they definitely never received any educational or medical support from them. The local VC were more in touch with the peasants in the hamlets than the government in Saigon was.

This was because of the power vacuum that resulted when the French departed and the South Vietnamese government took over. The French had had better control of the country and they supplied medical care to everyone, sometimes rounding up entire villages to inoculate them against diseases such as smallpox. But with the Viet Cong rebellion going on, the South Vietnamese government's control did not extend beyond the heavily populated areas. The outlying and backwoods areas, and the people living there, were left pretty much on their own.

Special Forces A-Teams were supposed to go out and try to change things. One of the ways of doing this was to conduct a MEDCAP (MEDical Civilian Assistance Program). We would send a medical team to a hamlet to treat the sick and distribute basic hygiene supplies such as soap, toothbrushes, and tooth paste. Naturally, we could not do MEDCAP while we were under attack, nor did we have the manpower to do one every week. But they were done regularly. The medical team would usually consist of

Author Jerry Krizan, seen at right in both photos, involved in a medical MEDCAP operation.

one of the Special Forces medics, some of the CID medics, a couple of the CID nurses, and an interpreter.

One time a MEDCAP was organized for a small hamlet two miles south of Loc Ninh. I had never been there before, even though it was close to our camp. We had a company-size operation in the field that had moved into the hamlet to secure it. This was supposed to be a "big deal public relations" MEDCAP, and the medical staff was helicoptered in. The staff consisted of the three camp nurses (they all wanted a ride in the helicopter); the senior CID medic; Nick, my interpreter; Lieutenant Jerry Toma, a Special Forces intelligence officer temporarily attached to our team; and myself. Actually, Toma was not his real name. His Army ID showed Toma, but he was working for the CIA at our camp and his identity had been changed.

A regular MEDCAP would treat any illnesses found, but was not normally well attended by the residents, except to receive the free stuff. Besides treating a few cases of ringworm, a cold or two, some minor infections—there was not much to do. But on this MEDCAP we wanted to try some-

thing a little different. It was going to be a "dental" MEDCAP operation. We were going to pull teeth. The general population did not receive any dental care whatsoever and an infected tooth would rot right down to the gum line. It must have been extremely painful to have a mouth full of such rotten teeth. The peasants liked to chew a small narcotic nut-like berry called Betel Nut. It was reddish in color and provided some pain relief. You could tell immediately who had bad teeth as they were always walking around spitting out red juice from the Betel Nut.

A helicopter picked up the medical team on the airstrip just outside camp and flew us the short distance. We landed and proceeded to organize our MEDCAP under a thatched-roofed, open-sided structure in the middle of the hamlet. Chairs were set up for patients to sit in while having their dental exams, and they were soon filled by some 30 of the locals. I examined the first one or two people and decided that the tooth they were complaining about needed to come out. As expected, the teeth were rotted down to the gum line and I did not think that they would be easy to pull. There was not much tooth left to grab a hold of with a universal dental forceps.

It was at this time I discovered that Nick had had a great deal of medic training before he became an interpreter. He was very good at giving shots

Dental MEDCAP, left to right: Senior CIDG medic, Lieutenant Toma, a Vietnamese, two Cambodian nurses, and author at far right.

Newly built MEDCAP house at CIDG dependent housing camp.

to deaden the area near a tooth. He was even very good at giving nerve block shots in the corner of the mouth to deaden one side of the lower jaw. At first, I wasn't sure how we were going to manage treating all the dental patients, but with Nick able to numb the teeth, things went a lot faster.

We set up an assembly line. A nurse examined a patient and identified the bad tooth. Then the patient would move to Nick's chair and he would give them a shot of lidocaine. As the anesthetic took effect I could see people touching their cheeks and mouth, experiencing a feeling of numbness they had never had before. They then sat themselves in my chair, I put on surgical gloves to protect myself, and I proceeded to pull the tooth.

It wasn't as difficult as I thought it would be, as the gum line was usually pretty much gone, so the tooth would come out roots and all. After I had extracted the tooth, I placed it in the patient's hands and passed them down to a medic who would give them a weeks' worth of penicillin to ward off any infection. Our little assembly line pulled over 30 teeth that day and relieved a lot of pain for those people who were in distress.

When it was over, we all posed for pictures. Even though they had never carried or fired any kind of weapon, the nurses wanted to have their picture taken holding a rifle, so we collected some from the CIDs. The chief CID medic, Lieutenant Toma, along with the three nurses and me stood in a line like a military unit facing the camera, each of us with a rifle at our side. It was good for a laugh. The helicopter returned and took us back to camp. We all felt pretty good because we had truly helped some people that day who would still be suffering if not for us.

CHAPTER 15

CAMP SANITATION

O NE OF THE MOST inglorious jobs of a medic on an A-Team in Vietnam was dealing with camp sanitation. Even though the primary emphasis of our training was medical in nature, we additionally received education in basic sanitation procedures. Sanitation covers a lot of areas ranging from insuring a potable water source to determining how the dishes in the kitchen were to be washed and dried. It also includes human waste disposal.

At left, three Vietnamese cleaning ladies; at right, two Cambodian nurses

The most highly trained MOS in Special Forces was Medical. The instruction period was longer and more difficult than for the other specialties, and most SF personnel did not possess the ability to complete the intense training sequence. I mean no disrespect to any of the other specialties, but they just could not do it. Among those joining Special Forces, only those with the highest IQ's were handpicked to be medics.

Myself, I wanted no part of it. I wanted to be a demo guy and blow stuff up but I did not have a choice. I was forced to become a medic. Apparently, in Vietnam the SF medics had such a high casualty rate that the Army needed all the replacements they could get. I don't know how I fooled them into thinking I was smart enough to be one, but they would not let go of me. And then I was a Special Forces Medic on an A-Team in Vietnam and in charge of sanitation along with all of my other medical duties.

———————

When I first arrived at Loc Ninh our only source of water was from a well in the old camp, about a quarter of a mile away. We had a water tanker truck that would run down to the old camp and then return to our current camp. We would fill up water cans all day long. For the inner compound we had 55 gallon drums welded together three high and four wide to hold our water for drinking, cooking, and showering. Into each truckload of water, the driver would add enough chlorine to choke a horse. It killed every living organism and tasted really bad.

One time someone got a "care package" from home with Kool-Aid and that seemed to help a little. I drank coffee with lots of sugar, which also helped to cut the foul taste. I never drank coffee before Vietnam, but after being in-country for a while I learned to like it. And eventually, even the regular water didn't taste too bad. My taste buds either adapted or had maybe died off from the chlorine. After we got a well dug in the camp, following the August 1968 siege, the water did not need as much chlorine and was somewhat better.

Anytime you went on a patrol you carried a couple canteens full of water. I always filled my canteens and froze them the night before an operation so I would have ice cold water for the first day out: a special treat on that initial day. When you were out in the field for three to five days there were no re-supplies unless it was an emergency ammo re-supply. You

One of two generators that supplied all the power for the camp.

had to live off the land and obtain your own water, which meant filling up your canteens at a stream and dropping in a couple water purification tablets. They made the water taste like shit but it was better than having the real shits for a week afterwards if you didn't use them.

Our team was on separate rations. That meant that neither the Army nor the B or C-Team furnished us with any food whatsoever. No daily grub or even C-rations were supplied for our operations. The LLDB and the CIDs got food flown in every two weeks on a C-130 or Caribou aircraft, which was unloaded on the airstrip outside camp. As we were on separate rations we were paid an extra $88.00 per month, though there were no grocery stores where we could pool our money and buy things for ourselves. We had to be industrious in trading with regular Army units to procure our food.

One of the high value trade items we had were captured enemy rifles—AK-47's and SKS's. We would trade them with supply personnel, or cooks in regular Army units, for cases of food, vegetables, potatoes, meats, C-rations—it didn't matter. The AK's looked totally cool, but because they were fully-automatic, you couldn't take them back to the States with you as war trophies. The SKS's, on the other hand, were semi-automatic and could be shipped back home to the USA and thus had a higher trade value than the AK's. By sending a scrounger back every month or so to Bien Hoa to buy beer and soft drinks and to trade for foodstuffs, our larder was always pretty well stocked.

We had a small kitchen next to the team room complete with a stove and an oven. The team room served as a dining hall and was where we kept the radio for contact with the operations in the field. To prepare the food we scrounged up, we had an old Papa-san who formerly cooked for the French when they were still around. We also had two old women who helped the Papa-san fix our meals and cleaned up afterwards.

One of the major points in kitchen sanitation was that in doing the dishes you washed them, rinsed them, and let them drip dry. But the two old women could not handle that. After rinsing the dishes they always wanted to attack them with one of their towels and dry them off. I was not there enough to enforce the "no dry rule," nor did I pay attention to what they were doing in the kitchen when I was there. As a matter of fact, with so much else of life and death importance going on most of the time, I wasn't even aware that I was in charge of sanitation in the kitchen. But one day we had a sanitation inspection and were written up because the inspector saw one of the old women touch a dish with a towel.

He let out a big whoop. I was told, "This is not acceptable and you will be in big trouble if you fail the inspection again."

The camp CO was very concerned, as it probably would look bad on his record if the team got written up for using a towel on a dish.

It didn't bother me. What were they going to do, send me to Vietnam? Besides I was off on another operation the next day and would not return for five days. Then I'd be two days in camp and back out again.

I did tell the old women that they could not dry the dishes with the towels even though I knew they would. I was out on patrol the next time an inspector came to camp, so I missed out on the next "Do not dry with towel" write up.

———

Rats were everywhere. I eventually began a campaign of "de-ratification" of the camp. First thing was to try to get rid of obvious sources, such as food scraps in the garbage. Second, we had two 12-gauge shotguns to utilize. I took out the buckshot from the rounds and replaced it with hard uncooked rice. This way I could shoot a rat inside a building without putting a hole in the wall. The rice did not penetrate the plywood panels when fired from about six feet away but it would stun a rat and let me get close enough for a kill shot with my second rice round. I killed a lot of rats. It was great sport.

About halfway through my tour the Army made us turn in our shotguns. Possessing shotguns might have been against some type of rule of warfare, but that was the end of my rat shooting for sport. Eventually I got two kittens from Loc Ninh to try and keep the rat population down. One died but the other grew up to be a great ratter. That cat definitely deserved some kind of medal.

So now I had lost my shotgun and couldn't practice my new sport. As a rule we did not carry M-16's around with us in camp, especially when everything was quiet and nobody was attacking us. I don't remember ever carrying my M-16 with me to conduct morning sick call at the dispensary. But the weapons guys had all kinds of other toys in the armory and I convinced them to issue me a .45 caliber pistol complete with a holster. I strapped it on and began to wear it whenever I was in camp. I felt like a cowboy. However, there were only two occasions when I actually fired that gun.

The first time, I was conducting a general sanitation inspection one day by walking around the inner perimeter of the camp while visually checking out the troops' wash areas, cooking facilities, and restrooms. At the southeast part of the camp, right by the airstrip, I spotted two young CIDs in the outer wire. They were crawling beneath the barbed wire through a little tunnel they had dug and were headed toward the airstrip. It looked like they were going AWOL, as the only other way out of camp was via the main entrance. I didn't particularly care if they were going AWOL but the little shits had made a secret pathway through the camp's defensive barrier. If they could sneak out by that means the enemy could just as easily sneak in the same way. I ran over to where they were and climbed on top of the berm wall. I drew my .45 and pointed it straight up into the air. At the top of my lungs I yelled "*Mot!*" (One!), and fired a round into the air. The shot was loud and echoed off the nearby barracks. The two guys looked back at me for a moment and then turned around and continued crawling under the wire.

I yelled *"Hai!"* (Two!), and fired off another round. They stopped and looked back at me again then kept on going. A crowd of CIDs had started to gather by this time to see what was happening.

I now yelled *"Ba!"* (Three), and aimed the .45 pistol at them. They looked back at me after I yelled *ba* and saw that the gun was pointed in their direction. They exchanged a couple of words between themselves and began to crawl back toward the camp, with me still leveling the .45 directly at them, until they reached the berm. They then ran back to their barracks. I went back and told one of our engineers (demo men) about the hole in the wire and it was promptly repaired.

The next and last time I ever fired my .45 was when it was my turn to drive to the airstrip to pick up the mail from our biweekly helicopter run. I grabbed some empty beer cans and tossed them into the jeep and drove it out the front gate to the tarmac where the chopper would land. Normally I would carry my M-16 when going anywhere outside of the camp but today I was packing my .45. The chopper had already radioed in and was about 15 minutes out. I had some time to kill so I set up the beer cans at the south edge of the tarmac, furthest away from camp, near the rubber trees.

I walked back about 30 feet then turned and took aim at the beer cans. I squeezed off three rounds but did not come close to hitting any of them. I took another three steps forward and carefully fired off three more rounds. None of them were close so I reloaded and moved closer until I was only about 10 feet away. In frustration I emptied the gun at the cans but still couldn't hit them.

The chopper landed, I grabbed the mailbag and put it into the jeep, and drove back to camp. I dropped off the mailbag in the team room then went and turned in my .45 caliber pistol. My gun slinging days were over. From then on, whenever I carried a weapon in the camp, it was always an M-16.

———————

Each CIDG company had its own individual restroom facilities. One type of elegant privy consisted of a four to six inch diameter metal tube stuck into a four to five foot deep hole in the ground with crushed rocks at the bottom. After the hole was filled in, the metal tube stuck out of the ground by another two feet and a layer of crushed rocks was scattered around its base and everywhere near it. The area was enclosed on three and a half sides by a four-foot wooden fence for the sake of privacy. This was the company "piss tube." Every day lime was dumped down the hole and spread over the rocks as a disinfectant and to keep the smell down. Unfortunately, most of the CIDs were not too accurate in their aim. And some of the Montagnards and Cambodians did not piss standing up anyway, preferring to squat. I have no idea how or if they used the tube, or if they were the ones responsible for the low hit-to-miss ratio at the base of the tube.

For the other bodily function, there was an old-time outhouse for each company. These outhouses accommodated multiple occupants with four or five holes for doing your business. Under each hole was a 55-gallon metal drum that had been cut in half to collect the fecal matter. Each day a poop squad would come by and replace the half-drums with clean ones. They then loaded up all the soiled half-drums, took them out of the camp, doused them with diesel fuel, and burned the contents. The next day they would come back and do the same thing and switch out the soiled half-drums. What a great job that was—hauling and burning shit!

The piss tubes and outhouses were not something that I checked on every day. They were not a high priority unless there was a problem, and I would not know there was a problem unless someone told me. One time the poop burners were complaining to their CID leader, who then complained to our team sergeant, who then informed me, that one of the companies was not properly using the poop holes. People were shitting on the floor and in between the seats and the poop squad was getting tired of cleaning it up. They were right. They should not have had to perform such a disgusting chore.

The next morning when the CIDs assembled in formation, I addressed the company that was shitting on the floor of their outhouse. I told them, "It is not going to be tolerated!" and thought that the problem was solved.

The next day the poop squad said that the problem was worse—that members of the company were still shitting all over the place. The following day I again addressed them at formation and they could tell I was getting pissed off. But those smart-asses kept it up for the next two days, continuing to shit all over the floor.

Finally, I told them, "If you don't stop it, I will burn your outhouse down."

I waited an extra day to make certain they had stopped, but they hadn't. They were basically saying, "Fuck you, *Bac Si*." I figured they had their chance and now it was my turn. I didn't intend to play fair when somebody was in my face and challenging my authority.

The outhouse in question was somewhat isolated and not near any other buildings. I got a five-gallon can of diesel fuel and another five-gallon can filled halfway with high-octane aviation fuel. I went into the outhouse and sure enough there was shit everywhere. I splashed half of the can of diesel fuel inside the outhouse and the other half on the outside. I splashed the aviation fuel on the sides. I was especially careful with the aviation fuel as that stuff is highly flammable and I was only using it for ignition purposes. I took out my Zippo and lit the side of the outhouse.

Poof! The fire quickly spread all over the outside and inside of the small structure. I had thought the diesel fuel would do a good job and I was right. The shitter burned intensely for several minutes, with flames rising up more than 10 feet into the air and producing a great deal of heat. All that was left was a pile of glowing, smoking coals where the outhouse had stood.

Mission accomplished.

Top asked me later in the day, knowing full well what I had done, "So what have you been up to *Bac Si?*"

"Just taking care of a sanitation issue," I told him.

I figured it would serve as a word of warning to the CIDs—"Don't call someone's bluff that has access to aviation and diesel fuel."

I was then out on patrol for a five-day operation, and when I got back I learned the outhouse-less company was bitching because they had to walk so far to use another company's shitter. An adjacent company would not let them use theirs as they did not want to take a chance and have it burned down.

My exact words to that outhouse-less company were, "Tough shit."

CHAPTER 16

DRY SEASON / TYPHOID

BEFORE PROCESSING-OUT OF Fort Bragg to go to Vietnam, everyone had to have their shot cards updated which meant being immunized for tropical diseases such as typhoid. You went and got your shots, your card was updated, and you were off without ever thinking about those shots again unless you were a Special Forces Medic. We had received extensive training in tropical diseases, especially the ones for which we were being vaccinated and were likely to encounter and treat in Vietnam. And we learned that a lot of these diseases were spread due to poor sanitation.

Interior wall of the main medical bunker.

The year I spent in-country, Vietnam had a particularly dry season. Generally, there would be the monsoon season and the rest of the time it was hot, humid, and rainy. But during my year it was very dry for over a month. While on one particular mission, I recall looking over at a low-lying area in the jungle as we walked by, and noticing that the ground appeared to be black—it was a small depression that had once been filled with water but had since dried up. As I kept on looking, the ground also appeared to be moving. It was alive! The ground was covered with leaches and they were slithering around. It was very horrible looking and totally gross. We had continued on another 100 yards away from the depression when all of the CIDs stopped and started to check themselves out by lifting up their shirts and pulling down their pants. If they were checking themselves for leaches, I was going to do the same. I found one between my navel and private parts. Though I knew the proper medical procedure for removing a leach, I panicked and ripped it off.

Parts of the jungle, as well as the weeds and vegetation on the ground, were tinder-dry. One time we had been out on patrol for three days and realized that someone was following us, though not especially close. It was probably a couple of local VC trying to find out where we were going. Since there was no good place for us to set up an ambush for them in the deep jungle, we didn't pursue it. We eventually came upon a large grassy field and sat down slightly inside the wood line to rest. The vegetation in the jungle was brown and desiccated and there was a strong, steady breeze blowing back toward the direction we had just come from. As we moved out, my Zippo lighter and I set 10 small fires that burned up real good and began to spread into the jungle. It looked like it was going to be a really big fire and would give the guys who were following us something to think about.

The village of Loc Ninh and the CID dependent-housing camp, east of our camp, each had a central well. Every day the women would go to the well, draw water, and carry it home in big buckets. They all wore black silk pajama tops and pants. I was in the village one day watching them drawing the water when one of the women stepped five feet away from the well, spread her legs out, pulled up one leg of her black pajama pants, and urinated. When she was through urinating, she pushed her pants leg back down and went to the well to gather more water. I noticed that this was a common practice and that the women would all urinate close to the well.

The public restroom facilities in the village of Loc Ninh consisted of a wooden structure with four small compartments built over the river. The compartments were approximately four feet by four feet and six feet high with an overhead roof. Each had a door for privacy. The toilet consisted of a hole in the floor with the river five feet below. To relieve yourself, you went into the little compartment, closed the door, and squatted over the hole in the floor. Everything dropped right down into the river and sank or floated away. Upstream or downstream, it didn't matter, there were often children playing in the river and women washing their family's clothes. From my perspective as a Special Forces Medic, both of these unsanitary practices—urination close to the water supply and fecal material going into the river—were prime conditions allowing for the spread of disease.

During that especially arid season the smaller and shallower wells in the district began to dry up and all at once we began to get a number of CIDs who were very sick with high fevers and abdominal pain. They did not look like typical malaria cases however, as there was no jaundice.

One of the symptoms of typhoid is a rosy rash. Most of these patients had a rash that appeared to be reddish in color. Another symptom of typhoid is a painful abdomen. If one of these patients was lying on their back and I pushed down on the belly and let up very quickly, they would almost jump off the table in pain. It was almost like checking for a bad appendix, (rebound tenderness in the right-lower quadrant of the abdomen), except it was painful for them in the middle of the abdomen. Most, but not all, of these folks had the painful abdomen but no diarrhea. That was my final determinate for diagnosing typhoid. As they were really very sick and we had no facilities for overnight or long term care, I would order a medevac and get them off to a hospital so they could be properly treated.

The epidemic lasted for over a week and during that time I had medevac'd probably 20 CIDs and a couple of civilians from Loc Ninh. The estimate was that over 20 people had died from typhoid in Loc Ninh and the CIDs dependent-housing camp. After I had medevac'd six CIDs with typhoid-like symptoms I got a call on the radio the next day from an American doctor at the hospital where they had been sent.

Lieutenant Toma at CIDG dependent housing camp.

He started to yell at me and said, "You sent a patient to the hospital that did not have typhoid. You are being derelict in your duties for not screening and diagnosing the typhoid cases better."

I told him, "I do not have the facilities to run blood tests on so many cases." I then asked him, "What about the other five CIDs who do have typhoid that I just sent and the other 15 that were previously sent and the 20 or so locals who have died in the last week from typhoid?"

He was being a butt-head and said, "You need to get your act together and to properly diagnose the typhoid cases."

He pissed me off and I said, "I will continue to send out any cases that appear to be typhoid and if you don't like it you are welcome to come up to Loc Ninh and assist in diagnosing them."

I then told him, "With all due respect sir, f*** you!" and hung up.

CHAPTER 17

CLAYMORES, AMBUSHES, AND HAND GRENADES

O N A NORMAL PATROL we did not carry claymores. Claymores were directional, anti-personnel mines about eight inches long, five inches high, and an inch and a half wide. They were loaded with some 700 small steel balls packed into a layer of C-4 explosive and weighed about three and a half pounds apiece. When detonated, their slightly concave shape produced a fan-shaped curtain of small lethal projectiles that were dispersed up to a distance of 100 yards. Claymores mines were very effective for purposes of camp defense. We would position them in rows around the outer

Fire direction arrow (lower right corner), designed to indicate the direction that aircraft should fire during an attack on the camp.

perimeter where they could nearly decimate an attacking enemy force.

Claymores were carried into the field two to a bag that had a long strap that could be easily slung over your shoulder. They would be deployed to protect the perimeter of an operation that was set up in its overnight position. The problem was that the sheer number of mines necessary to do that effectively was way more than we wanted to lug. Another reason for not bringing them on our missions was that we would often hide in the woods or jungle for the night, and the claymores were not really needed because the VC or NVA were unable to find us. Also, the CIDs would sometimes open them up and steal the C-4 to use for cooking or to sell on the black market in town, thereby rendering them useless. As we had to tote everything on our backs on five-day missions, the extra weight of the claymores was usually not worth it.

I know I did not like to carry them into the field. The thought of a stray bullet hitting a claymore during a firefight and blowing up while on my hip did not give me a warm fuzzy feeling.

———————

The times that we did carry claymore mines were during multi-company operations, and one of our primary objectives was to launch an ambush, usually at night. We might be conducting a general recon of a certain area with orders to set one up on a particular trail. Or, on small recon patrols we sometimes carried a couple of claymores. They were easy to detonate by means of a trip wire on the trail behind us if we believed we were being followed.

Reconnaissance patrols only lasted three days, so carrying the extra weight of a couple of claymores was not as bad as having to haul them around for five days. But with only 30 or fewer CIDs on a recon patrol, setting up ambushes was typically not one of our primary objectives. We were supposed to scout around and see if we could spot any enemy, or signs of them, and if possible identify their units and probable strength. The best way to identify a unit of the NVA was to kill or capture one of its soldiers, then examine the insignia on his uniform. Because on recon we were heading right into the area where the bad guys were, we were generally outnumbered and out gunned.

There were a couple of times on recon we did use claymores to set up an ambush. One time we were proceeding alongside a well-worn trail that the NVA were probably using for infiltration, and we could tell that someone was behind us. To infiltrate undetected the NVA typically moved around in groups of three to six. We quietly positioned five CIDs in the foliage along the west side of the trail and put in place two claymores aimed back down the trail and another one directly in front of the CIDs facing the trail broadside. Though the area was fairly open, it was still the best spot to set up an ambush. Since we could not all remain in the immediate area, the rest of us continued on for another 40 yards then sat down and waited. We thought that the CIDs we had left behind would be able to handle a group of three to six NVA, especially with the claymores in place. Also, we were close enough to move up and support the ambush, and catch the enemy in a cross fire if necessary.

It wasn't long before I heard a "Boom, Boom, Boom!" as the CIDs blew the claymores. The rest of us immediately got up and started to move on line toward the ambush site. There was some gunfire ahead of us, and then all was quiet. As we approached, the CIDs were standing up and pointing across the trail. Apparently, what happened was that three NVA were walking down the trail toward the ambush site and one of the CIDs panicked and set off his claymore too soon; the other CIDs then detonated theirs as well. The bad guys had not been completely into the kill zone when the claymores went off and they ran into the jungle on the other side of the trail. The CIDs said that two of them had been hit and the other one was running with a real bad limp. We did spot a couple drops of blood on the trail and a few more leading into the jungle, but as the NVA were not within the maximum effective range of the mines' forward blast area, they were probably only struck by some stray pellets.

Not a completely successful ambush, but it would probably spook the bad guys for a while not knowing what might lie ahead, on this and every other trail they walked on. There was nothing more we could do here and we knew that any other NVA nearby would soon be coming to check out what had happened. Since they probably greatly outnumbered us, we got the hell out of the area.

I was only on a couple of night ambush operations, both of them more or less the same. We placed M-60 machine guns on either end of an ambush area to be able to have overlapping fire crisscrossing the killing zone. A couple of claymores were then positioned so that the arc of their front-blast area would also crisscross the trail. The claymores, if properly aimed, would devastate anything in their path. Other claymores were placed parallel to the ambush site and pointed directly at the killing zone along the path. The CIDs were deployed in a box formation with the majority of them on line at the ambush site behind the claymores. The rest would be protecting the machine guns at the ends of the formation or safeguarding our flanks and rear.

We moved quietly into the ambush site right before dusk and got into our positions. Then it was a matter of lying there, trying to stay still and not make any noise for what seemed like an eternity. The hours slowly passed and it would be all you could do to stay awake. Many of the CIDs were dozing off, with others gently nudging them awake. Even I had trouble keeping awake and often found myself nodding off after midnight. Around three or four in the morning we gave up on the ambush, with the majority of us falling asleep while a couple of CIDs kept watch. It was very boring. Neither of my company-sized operation night ambushes ever yielded anything. They just turned out to be long sleepless nights.

One thing I did in preparation for night ambushes, or any kind of night engagement, was to load some tracer rounds in a couple of magazines for my M-16. Every third round I loaded would be a tracer. Regular M-16 bullets were bronze in color at the point, while the tracer rounds were a dull silver color at the point.

The key to winning a fire fight with the enemy was to get them to duck and keep their heads down and not return fire. If their heads were down, then our troops were more likely to be able to remain composed and lay down an accurate field of fire which would then force the enemy to either stay down or to disengage and run off. I don't care who you are, if there are bullets cracking over your head and hitting all around you, you have a natural tendency to get down to protect yourself. In the daylight the tracer rounds can't be seen, but when they are fired at night they really light up their pathway. Even though the enemy can better get a fix on your position, I put in a tracer in every third round so I could see where my own gunfire was going, as I wanted to keep it low and directed at the bad guys. I also wanted to let them know that when they saw the tracer rounds whizzing by, they were being fired upon—a reality that might cause them to lose their nerve and reduce the accuracy of their return fire.

Grenades were something that we would not let the CIDs carry on any operation. We just didn't trust them with a grenade. They threw like girls. No, I take that back—any American girl can throw a whole lot better than they could. Growing up in America, a boy or girl would have had some experience tossing a baseball or football around, but in Vietnam they had never played any sport that required throwing a ball. They could chuck a baseball only about 10 feet. That would not work for grenade tossing, as you would have a better chance of blowing up yourself and your buddies than you would the enemy.

Even though we were on separate rations, meaning that the Army did not and would not supply us with any kind of foodstuffs, we could order all kinds of non-food related items and within a week or so it would show up on our little airstrip, delivered to us by a C-130 or Caribou transport plane. Someone on the Team got the bright idea that we should order some sports equipment so we could teach the CIDs how to throw. Maybe if they learned how to toss baseballs and footballs we could show them how to toss hand grenades. The Army sent us a couple of footballs, some baseball equipment, and a volleyball set. I took it upon myself to try to play catch with a football with the CIDs in camp. The CIDs not only could not throw, they had no concept of how to catch a football. After a couple weeks of working with them and trying to instruct them on how to do it, I gave up. They simply did not get it and no progress was ever made in developing their skills. So no grenades for them.

Volleyball was something else. They liked playing volleyball and were pretty good at it. A couple of teammates and I would sometimes play in their games. Due to my (at least) ten-inch height advantage, I should have been a star volleyball player, but the CIDs were always calling me for fouls of some sort. The major foul was when I hit a ball below my waist and used my open hand to strike it. According to their rules, any ball at or below the waist had to be punched with closed fists. As my instinct was always to hit the ball with my hands, they decided they did not want to play volleyball with me anymore. So in football I was on the "All-Vietnam-ese Team," and in volleyball no one wanted to play with me.

A couple of the CIDs did learn to toss the football a little, but not good enough to toss a grenade. As far as trying to get them to play a game of baseball or touch football to improve their skills, the whole concept was completely alien to them.

CHAPTER 18

CAMP DEFENSES AND ATTACKS

THE A-TEAM AT LOC Ninh was located in a unique area of South Vietnam. Our area of operations jutted slightly into Cambodia where the North Vietnamese Army had free reign. They could stage their troops there before moving across the border to attack whatever South Vietnamese or American target they had selected. A lot of the other A-Teams located near the border of Cambodia would observe a great deal of activity and have contact with the NVA as well. But once the NVA had infiltrated into South Vietnam and moved out of a camp's AO to attack larger targets to the south, things might get relatively quiet for three, four, or even six months while there was no enemy present. Some A-Teams did have a lot of activity from local VC, but at Loc Ninh we had very little. The VC in our area had been reduced to a non-effective fighting force. The only attacks we had on our camp, and most of the contact we had with the enemy during operations, was with hardcore NVA soldiers.

During the year I was at Loc Ninh we had two major attacks on our camp by North Vietnamese troops, in August and September 1968. The primary objective of the NVA at that time was to concentrate on hitting and overrunning us, but it appeared that after September, the focus of the NVA shifted to targets further south around Bin Hoa and Saigon. Even though they were not hitting us as a primary target, our camp would still be attacked with mortars and rockets as the enemy passed by on its way south. Whether it was a diversionary tactic to get US Army Intelligence to think they were now concentrating on us, or just their way of saying "Hi" as they moved through our AO, we never knew. We sometimes joked at the camp that we were only there for NVA training purposes, to give them some live combat experience they could use against us later. We were hit at least once a month as they honed their skills on us.

I don't mean to make light of these assaults on the camp because their intention was to kill as many of us as possible, and if a weakness developed in our defenses, to overrun us. The only thing the NVA would no longer attempt was massive charges by their troops upon our perimeter. But due to the almost continuous threat posed by the enemy we still had to be on a combat readiness status at all times.

The design of the camp at Loc Ninh was in a diamond shape, which was a very efficient configuration for repelling ground assaults by the NVA. Strands of concertina barbed wire laced with trip flares surrounded the camp. Claymore mines were set in front of the berm, which was a four-foot deep, slightly elevated trench. The berm enabled the CIDs to be able to stand upright and fire their weapons. At the points of the diamond shape and along the berm there were reinforced concrete machine gun bunkers to provide cross fire against any advancing enemy troops. And located just within the berm at the points of the diamond were mortar pits, which combined with the three pits located in the inner compound to deliver a deadly mortar barrage. Two South Vietnamese 105mm howitzers were located on the north west side of the camp for additional firepower. The 105's would be used to fire directly into the advancing enemy. Even the CIDs above-ground barracks were strategically positioned to be no more than 10 to 20 feet from the berm. During an attack this would cause the CIDs to rush to their defensive positions on the berm and in the machine gun bunkers—which were a whole lot safer places to be than hiding in barracks that provided no protection from mortars.

The inner compound buildings that housed the team members and the LLDB were three-quarters underground, but not protected against direct hits from enemy artillery. Only the commo bunker and the medical bunker had hardened reinforced roofs to safeguard them from direct mortar or rocket hits. Each team member had an assigned position to go to during an attack. The senior communications specialist and the CO were in the commo bunker to oversee the defense of the camp and to request help from the B-Team if required. The senior medic was assigned to the medical bunker and the two weapons guys were generally assigned to the inner compound's mortar pits. The juniors in rank, along with the other teammates, were assigned to defensive positions on the berm or in machine gun bunkers where they could call in with their handheld radios to direct fire on the enemy, and to help coordinate the defense of the camp.

As part of our general preparedness we rotated two-hour night watch shifts on a radio in the team room. To help stay awake and to maintain camp security, we checked in with the B-Team every hour. We had someone on the radio at all times in case one of our operations in the field got into contact and needed support. It was also advisable to go out to a couple of different spots in the berm to make sure that the CIDs on night watch were actually awake. You would let the B-Team know that you were going out for an inspection, and once you returned you would radio the B-Team that everything was okay and you were back on the air.

My first defensive position when I arrived at Loc Ninh was in the mortar pit in the inner compound. As a junior in rank—sergeant—I shared a two-man room with another teammate. The CO, XO, Top, and the SFC's all had private quarters. One time during an attack when I was in the mortar pit firing illumination mortar rounds, the room I shared took a direct hit from an enemy mortar. It blew the crap out of it and tore up some of my things including pictures and a spare green beret. If I had been in there when the round detonated it would have been lights out for me, but fortunately I had already raced out to the mortar pit.

———————

When I became the senior medic as a Sergeant E-5, my post was the medical bunker. It was one of the safest places to be in the camp. The medical bunker was safe from mortars but during an attack there was nothing to do but wait, as it was dangerous to move around the compound. Once the main barrage was over I knew the casualties were going to arrive. In the meantime, I would use the time to insure that everything was ready including having field dressings and IV's laid out. As soon as the CID medics started bringing in their wounded comrades the nurses would all scurry into the bunker. Only during the August and September attacks of 1968 did we have a large number of casualties. Otherwise there were only a few minor shrapnel wounds.

Both the communications and medical bunkers had an advantage that none of the other teammates' sleeping quarters had. They were air conditioned to keep the radio equipment from overheating and medications from spoiling. The senior commo man and the senior medic slept in their respective bunkers and therefore had air conditioned comfort at night. The medical bunker was a large bunker as far as bunkers go. It was about 30 feet wide by 40 feet long. It was large enough to hold two operating tables, a couple of medicine supply cabinets, and had an area spacious enough for treating five or six personnel at once, as well as accommodating my bunk in the rear corner.

A problem was that when casualties came in we would have the wounded, the CID medics, the nurses, and some of the wounded CIDs' buddies all in the medical bunker at once. One time after everyone had been treated and the bunker was empty I went back to rest on my bunk and noticed that about half of my personal items were missing. During the confusion someone had ripped me off. The next day I got the camp carpenter to build an 8- by 10-foot plywood-sided room with a lockable door in the far corner of the bunker for my bunk and personal items. Problem solved.

In the mornings we would all usually meet up in the team room to get coffee, have some breakfast, and see if Top had anything special for us to do that day. One morning I came in and poured some coffee as other team members started to filter in. They all looked tired and were talking about the mortar attack the previous night.

As they were going over what had happened I asked, "What mortar attack?"

A couple of them said to me "Quit BS'ing, *Bac Si*."

I said, "It's no BS, I didn't hear any mortar attack."

A couple others said, "Very funny *Bac Si!*"

Then someone else remarked, "I don't remember seeing him at all last night." Others chimed in that they hadn't seen me either. Eventually none of them could remember seeing me the night before.

As it turns out, I had slept through a devastating mortar attack that had lasted for about 45 minutes.

I was on a multi-company operation and we were settled in for the night in the woods about four miles from Loc Ninh. Around midnight we could hear explosions and see flashes of light coming from the direction of the camp. We radioed in and asked, "What's going on?"

"We are getting hit from the north side near the rubber trees," was the response.

We asked, "What do you want us to do? Do you want us to return and assist?"

The camp replied, "No, stay where you are for now but be ready at first light to come back. Take a southerly route as the bad guys are all to the north side."

We settled in for the night feeling frustrated that there was nothing we could do to help our teammates. But they were right, if we tried to move toward the camp and made contact with the enemy there would be nothing they could do to support us, as they were already engaged. Also, in the dark we would more than likely be shot at by some of our own jumpy troops as we neared the camp. So we stayed put. At first light we got the CIDs to move out. We covered the four miles or so in about two hours without seeing any bad guys along the route we took to just south of the camp.

Burned-out LLDB barracks after being hit by mortars.

As we rolled through the main gate we could see major destruction. The LLDB barracks on the left side of the gate to the inner compound was gone. It had been completely blown apart and was now nothing but a pile of burned boards with sandbags strewn around. When we reported in, Top said, "We are really glad to see you because if the NVA had found you out there they would have ripped you a new one and we need the help here."

After I ditched my backpack and gear in my room, I went to the team room to catch up on what had happened. A couple of my teammates were in there and asked me, "Did you see the LLDB barracks? They bombed it."

"What do you mean they bombed it?"

"A MIG flew over and dropped a bomb on us."

It could have been possible for a North Vietnamese MIG to fly low, hugging the border of Cambodia and penetrate eight or so miles into South Vietnam and drop a bomb, but I doubted it. I'm not sure the NVA, during the course of the war, ever attacked any targets in South Vietnam from the air. Because it was on a night when the camp did not have any American air support that could have mistakenly hit us, the only explanation for some was that it was a MIG. I still don't believe it, but I know a couple of my old teammates continue to think they survived a MIG attack!

CHAPTER 19

NEW DIRECTIONS OF THE WAR

S IX MONTHS OR SO into my tour the nature of the war in Vietnam began to change. Our new directives involved a new operational approach, initiated at the highest levels by the commanders of US Armed Forces. I believe some of these changes may have started earlier but it took a while for things to filter down to us, near the bottom of the food chain. The regular American troops were at the top of the chain for support and supply, as well they should be; next came the South Vietnamese Army (ARVN); followed by the RFPF (Regional Forces Popular Forces); and finally us—the Special Forces A-Teams.

The new strategy for pursuing the war in Vietnam involved the South Vietnamese Army taking on a more active role in the fight against the invading North Vietnamese Army. The ARVN was to be trained to a higher level of combat readiness, receive updated arms and ammunition, and with the assistance of American advisors, take over actual combat operations from American troops. As they never operated in our AO when I was at Loc Ninh I can't comment on their level of readiness or effectiveness.

The process for us meant that our indigenous troops were issued new M-16 rifles. The M-16's were fully-automatic weapons as opposed to the semi-automatic M-1 carbines, M-2 carbines, and old M-1's that they had been using. The CIDs were now competitive with the NVA or VC who all had AK-47's that were fully automatic and held a 30-round clip. Our troops could respond with M-16's on full-automatic with 20-round clips. Previously it had not been an even match; most of the CIDs were firing their semi-automatic rifles (bang, bang, bang, bang) while the bad guys were ripping off 30 rounds in the same amount of time.

NEW DIRECTIONS OF THE WAR • 141

The troops also received additional M-60 machine guns and M-79 grenade launchers that gave them enhanced fire power on our missions. The M-60 was a great improvement from the guns they turned in: Korean War or WWII A-4 or A-6, .30 caliber machine guns. The old 30 Cals were so heavy that none of the CIDs could carry them in the field. And the M-79 grenade launchers were on par with the RPG rocket launchers that the bad guys carried.

We began to receive new dictates for our field operations, which at the time I thought were the result of directives from the top Army leadership. As I would subsequently learn, they were actually due to a change in command at the B-Team level. The new B-Team CO, a lieutenant colonel, did not have any Special Forces experience and was unfamiliar with A-Team operations.

For one thing we were ordered to shave every day. I guess we did look pretty grubby when we came in from a five-day patrol, but there was no way we could shave in the field. We were spending the night in hammocks in the jungle and carrying all our supplies in backpacks. Nevertheless, we were now told to carry some type of shaving kit and mirror while on a mission. It didn't make any sense at all. We smelled pretty bad too from not having bathed for five days when we came in, but the new orders did not address that issue.

In addition, we were ordered to carry C-4 in the field and blow up any bunker complexes we found. There were extensive bunker complexes all over our AO, some were new and many were old. We would not have been able to carry enough C-4 with us to blow up even one complex, much less all of them. It would have taken a ton of C-4 to do that. If we found a bunker complex on an operation we would normally destroy it by tearing it apart and having everyone shit in the holes—our special greetings to the visiting NVA troops. We turned it from a bunker complex to a shit hole.

But orders were orders.

Okay. Check. Carry C-4 to blow up the complexes. Shave every day from the comfort of your hammock. Right!

Sometimes you just had to salute and say, "Yes sir," then go on about your business as usual. We never did blow up a bunker complex or shave while in the field.

A third new directive was that all of our patrols were now to be out of

Mortar ammo being unloaded and stored.

mortar and/or artillery range of the camp. Previously, any time we had contact with the enemy on an operation we could call in mortar or artillery fire on the bad guys' position and it could change the direction of the battle in our favor. Being out of range would really hurt us. If there were more of our troops than there were enemy troops, we would probably be okay, even if we took more casualties than we would have if we were able to call in artillery and mortars on their position. But if we ran into a larger group of bad guys we probably wouldn't have a chance, as the hardcore NVA troops were a lot better trained, more disciplined, and braver than our CIDs on a man-to-man basis. We might not lose too badly though, as the CIDs would cut and run like hell to save themselves if they knew they were outnumbered.

If we were within mortar and artillery range of the camp and could call in fire on the enemy, in the best case it would inflict some harm on them, and in the worst case it would hold them off while we ran like hell to get away. We could also call in airstrikes on the enemy, but because we were on the bottom of the list for this type of support, this option was not always available to us. If an American or South Vietnamese unit was in

4.2-inch mortar with mortar rounds, in main mortar pit.

contact with the enemy at the same time, the South Vietnamese would receive air support from helicopter gunships or Air Force jets. We would be on our own.

So it seemed to us that with this one new order, we had given up the one tactical advantage we had over the enemy, and they had not given up a thing. And it was made worse by the fact that the NVA soldiers were a lot better than ours and were 100% committed to winning. Our troops' main concern was to survive, no matter how hard we trained them to fight.

Cambodia was approximately nine miles to the north and 10 miles to the west of our camp at Loc Ninh. We were on a mission in a part of Vietnam that jutted into Kampong Cham Province near the so-called Fish Hook area. The mission's objective was to patrol north of the rubber plantation that extended six miles north of us, and to recon in the jungle that ran all the way to the border and beyond. The enemy was all over this area, as the Fish Hook was a major terminus point along the Ho Chi Minh Trail. The NVA and the VC maintained bases there and considered it to be their home territory. Our Intelligence believed that COSVN (Central Office for South Vietnam), the NVA's political and military headquarters, was located in the Fish Hook. And we were going right up to their doorstep without mortar or artillery support!

Each American team member on the patrol carried a map of our AO. We paid close attention to it to make sure we knew where we were in case we had to call in artillery or air support. I did not look at my map continuously, but checked it every half hour or so or whenever we stopped. We would walk about three klicks between stops, and by looking at my compass I had a good idea of where we were and which way we were going. Each time we stopped I would confer with my teammate to be certain of our location. I was pretty good at map reading but you couldn't always trust these particular ones, which were old French maps. It was also very difficult at times to know exactly where you were. There were no major landmarks, such as rivers or hills, that you could use to orient yourself in the jungle—those elements looked the same wherever you were.

We continued heading further up into the jungle and then turned slightly to the west. I was getting concerned as I thought we were getting too close to the border. As a matter of fact, I thought that we might have crossed it already.

At our next stop I questioned the LLDB and CID company commanders and they both said, "No sweat *Bac Si*, no Cambodia."

"Bullshit!" I told my teammate. "I think we are there."

It wasn't like there were markers or signs posted saying "Welcome to Cambodia," or a fence in the jungle separating the two countries. Where we were, north of the rubber plantation, was all wild and unexplored wilderness stretching for miles and miles.

After the break we started walking slightly to the northwest and had gone only about a klick when the CIDs began freaking out. The entire jungle in front of us was full of tank tracks. They went every which way. My first thought was that the 11th Cav must have been up here recently, but they hadn't been in our AO for quite a while and these tracks looked like they were only a day or two old. The CIDs were ready to *didi mau* out of there.

I pointed to the tank tracks.

"American?"

"No, no *Bac Si*—VC tank!" they insisted.

I didn't have any idea what the difference was between an American tank track and an NVA tank track, which would have been from a Russian supplied tank. But the CIDs were convinced that these belonged to the enemy.

I made a quick mental inventory. We had 140 CIDs with M-16's, a couple of M-60 machine guns, and possibly a couple of LAW's (Light Anti-tank Weapons). It was questionable if the CIDs would know how to fire a LAW, especially at a tank that was firing at them. Because of these factors, combined with the lack of mortar or artillery support from the camp, (we were out of range anyway), I agreed with the CIDs this time. It was better to live to fight another day. We should leave the area immediately.

We reported our position, status and findings back to camp. The transmission went something like this:

"Muggy Caucus, Muggy Caucus (the camp's call sign)—this is Muggy Caucus Kilo (my call sign)."

After they responded I said, "Muggy Caucus, we have fresh Romeo-Uncle-Sierra-Sierra-India-Alfa-Nancy (RUSSIAN) tank tracks and we are getting the hell out of here, over and out."

We immediately headed south back into Vietnam and away from the tank tracks. That was the first and last time I was ever in Cambodia, and it was strictly by accident.

Intelligence already suspected the NVA had Soviet bloc-supplied tanks in their sanctuaries in Cambodia and we had confirmed it. They were probably some of the same NVA tanks that in 1972 overran what was the former Special Forces camp at Loc Ninh, and participated in the attack on the military base at An Loc to the south that had housed our former B-Team headquarters. This was after the US had withdrawn most of its combat troops from Vietnam.

CHAPTER 20

HELICOPTER ATTACK

————————

I WAS RUNNING AN OPERATION in the southeast part of our AO. It had been raining off and on for a couple of days. The rain poured down in buckets and came from every which way. We were all wearing our ponchos and while they kept one's head, shoulders, and hips dry, the blowing rain running off the poncho soaked your jungle fatigues below the knees and caused your feet to slosh around inside your jungle boots. You would be walking along going slosh, slosh, slosh in the reddish clay mud. Then when the rain stopped the air would be so humid it felt like you could slice through it with a knife. After the sun came out we would still be sloshing in our boots through the red mud, but then dust from the patches of dried red clay soil would start to blow in our faces. It was just a miserable set of conditions but onward we went, only stopping to eat and rest, while trying to dry out. We had been trudging through the wet humid jungle for two days when we stopped to check out an abandoned hamlet.

All of the 20 or so mud brick huts were empty with their roofs caved in. It was a very scenic location however, on top of a small hill surrounded by the jungle. There was a main well in the middle of the hamlet from which our troops were refilling their canteens, and as it was noon we decided to eat lunch and rest. During the course of the war the South Vietnamese government had forced many residents of outlying hamlets, such as this one, to move to larger population centers. That way the peasants would not be intimidated by the local VC and forced to supply food and manpower. This place looked like it was the result of one of those forced relocations.

Troops were positioned all around the perimeter of the hamlet for protection, and had started to relax after eating lunch when two American helicopters were spotted flying in our direction. A few of the troops stood up to wave when, from just inside the jungle, a couple of VC, who must have been following us, opened up on the choppers with their AK-47's. The CIDs at the edge of the hamlet then opened up in the direction of the VC who were shooting at the helicopters. The VC quit shooting and ran off. They had not hit the helicopters, but all that the helicopter crews could see was our people out in the open, firing their weapons. Everything had happened so fast that the crews could not tell that the gunfire aimed at them had come from the jungle and not from us.

First of all, helicopters were not supposed to be flying here at all, as it was not a free fire zone for them. It was our AO and we were patrolling it. But when these helicopters took ground fire they responded by opening up on us! The two birds made a pass over the hamlet while firing their M-60 machine guns, despite some of the CIDs and myself trying to wave them off. But we all had to take cover as they continued to shoot at us. From the air we probably looked like a VC unit as much as we looked like a CIDG unit.

I got down behind a crumbling half-wall from an out building and got on the PRC-25 and radioed back to camp. I shouted into the handset, "We are getting hit by a couple of American helicopters! Get them off our ass!"

I had no idea what the choppers' radio frequency was, so I had no way to contact them. The camp at Loc Ninh was frantically calling the B-Team, trying to get hold of someone who could make radio contact with the helicopters and make them stop firing.

And now they were circling back toward us for another gun run. This time we all dove for cover behind the mud brick walls of the empty huts. During all of this I was on the radio back to camp telling them, "They are coming at us again!"

The machine gun bullets were hitting everywhere. I began to think we were not going to get out of this alive. Taken out by American helicopters. What a way to go!

At this point I had no idea what our casualties might be, though I assumed they had to be significant. My only concern was to stay on the radio to camp and get these guys off us.

The choppers were turning and getting ready for a third strafing run when I told the camp, "Get those mother F***ers off my ass or I'll shoot them down myself!"—which I was ready to do. I'd blow those birds from the sky if I had to. At this point it was kill or be killed.

The helicopters were about to start firing again when they suddenly veered off. They must have received word over their radio that they were shooting at "friendlies." Without any acknowledgement to us, they turned and flew to the south and were soon out of sight.

My thoughts were: *Thanks a lot guys for admitting your mistake and taking responsibility and seeing if we needed any help.*

Now it was time to see what they had done to us. I believed it might be really bad, with multiple wounded or even KIA. After all the machine gun fire we took I was sure that we would have several casualties, but when I checked with the troops we only had one—a CID had been hit on the canteen that he wore on his right hip. The M-60 round destroyed the canteen but did not touch him at all except to leave a big black and blue mark. It probably hurt like hell but we didn't notice. All of the CIDs, including Mr. Wounded Canteen, and I, were laughing like crazy either from nerves or because it was so damned funny.

I reported our status back to the team. They were anxious to hear from us and were wondering how bad we had been hit and what our casualties were. I could hear Top in the background still screaming at whoever he had on the radio about the choppers attacking us in our AO. My report was something like, "One casualty, and one canteen KIA," followed by much laughter from me. It was a good thing for us the door gunners on those birds couldn't shoot straight.

The CIDs had been good at hiding and avoiding being hit, but we were also extremely lucky. We briefly looked around in the immediate area of the hamlet for the bad guys who had taken pot shots at the helicopters, but they were long gone. All of that machine gun fire, even though it wasn't directed at them, must have scared them off.

And then it was time to pack up and go back to beating down the jungle as we moved on to our next objective.

CHAPTER 21

CHINESE CLAYMORES

F EBRUARY 15, 1969, IS one of the few actual dates during my tour in
Vietnam that I can identify for certain. I was on a five-day, multi-company operation with SFC Merley Maynard. We had been out in the jungle
east of Village 2 and south of Highway 14 for four days tramping in the
heat and humidity, and had not found anything of importance. We did
shoot at a couple of VC on day two but the rest of the time was dull and
boring.

SFC Merley Maynard instructing a lieutenant on how to hand fire a 60mm mortar.

By this time on my tour I would carry a couple of paperback books in the pockets of my jungle fatigue pants to read while in the field. On a typical operation we would walk for a couple of hours, rest for a half hour, walk for a couple of hours, then take an hour for lunch. In the afternoon we would again walk, rest, walk, rest, stop for dinner, and then move to an overnight location. There was plenty of down time spent sitting around, and I would read my books then. War, as it turns out, really was days of boredom followed by minutes of excitement and terror.

Though my nickname on the team was *Bac Si* and everyone called me that, especially the CIDs, after I had been out with Maynard on a couple of missions and we had gotten into some firefights with the bad guys, he said he was changing my nickname to "Contact."

Whenever we engaged with the enemy we would radio in to the camp using the current monthly call sign. An example would be "Muggy Caucus, Muggy Caucus (the A-Team call sign)—this is Muggy Caucus Kilo (the call sign for me—Krizan). We have contact." I would then describe the situation and let them know what kind of support we required.

Maynard was already joking about my new nickname the night before. I started to think he was right, as I could not remember a three-day recon patrol or a five-day, multi-company operation during which we did not engage with the enemy. I might not have personally fired my weapon every single time, but there was always contact of some sort with them.

When we had stopped for the last night we were still maybe a half-day's walk through the bush and rubber from the camp. I had been in-county for nine months and my camouflage hat and fatigues were pretty well bleached out from being washed so many times. They looked just like the fatigues the CIDs wore, which allowed me to blend in easily with them and not look so American, even though I was much taller.

But I had made several changes to my gear over time. I now carried a soft canvas backpack rather than the one issued which had a metal frame and was too heavy. The canvas backpack held my hammock, poncho, poncho liner, toothbrush and toothpaste, spare socks, a quarter stick of C-4 for cooking, rations for four days, and a roll of toilet paper. I knew we would usually return to camp at noon on the fifth day, so carrying extra rations wasn't necessary. I also carried only two canteens of water, which would last for the duration. In the beginning of my tour I brought five filled canteens on each mission and was drinking like a camel. But after I was acclimatized I didn't need that much water.

I no longer wore a web ammo belt. Instead, I carried my ammo in two claymore bags—one slung over my right shoulder resting on my left hip, and one tied around my waist resting on my right hip. The bag on my left hip was a comfortable place for my left arm when holding the stock of my M-16. I could hold the stock in my left hand with my right hand grasped around the pistol grip of the rifle. The thumb of my right hand was on the safety while my right index finger was alongside the trigger. It was comfortable to carry the M-16 this way and it was always ready to go. If we got hit or were ambushed, all I had to do was point the rifle at the bad guys, flick off the safety with my thumb, and put my index finger on the trigger. In less than a second I could be firing on full-automatic. Some guys were lazy and carried their weapon over their shoulder or walked along holding it in one hand. Their reaction time would not be as fast in getting the first shot off. I always wanted to be ready to return fire ASAP.

On day five of the operation we had walked for nearly half an hour when the CIDs got on the main east-west route through the jungle, which was roughly 30 feet of cleared foliage with a one-rut trail in the middle. Maynard and I were concerned about walking on the trail, though it was a whole lot easier than beating our way through the bush. The CIDs assured us, "No sweat *Bac Si*, no VC." We were nearing the end of a boring mission and got lazy I guess. We all started walking west on the trail toward the rubber trees.

Approximately a klick and a half from the edge of the plantation there were two large explosions to our left on the south side of the trail, and then automatic rifle fire coming at us from the tree line beyond. The explosions were from Chinese claymores being set off by the enemy. I was knocked sideways and went down on my right knee. The CIDs returned fire and began to fall back toward the opposite tree line on the north side of the trail. I immediately opened fire on full-automatic and went through two clips before I realized what had happened.

We had been ambushed.

In our procession, Maynard and his radio man had been walking directly in front of me and my radio man was right behind me. I looked toward Maynard and he was down on the ground and trying to get up. His radio man had already made it to the tree line on the right side of the trail. My radio man was on the ground hiding behind me, and as he started to get up to run toward the protection of the trees, I grabbed him and held him with me and kept firing on full-automatic. The rounds from my M-16 were chewing up the foliage in front of me where I thought the bad guys might be hiding.

I ran over to Maynard in a half-crouched position while continuing to shoot toward the trees on the south side of the trail. He was up on his hands and knees and started a fast crawl on all fours toward the tree line. I moved along behind him, still in my half-crouched position and still firing my M-16 to cover him, as we both scrambled to the safety of the tree line where the CIDs were maintaining a heavy volume of return fire. Once we were inside the tree line I checked on Maynard. He seemed to be coming around after being knocked down and out from the concussion of the two Chicom (Chinese) claymores. He had a small wound on his hand but other than being dazed, he seemed okay.

I grabbed my radio man and took the handset of the radio in my left

Lt. Buck, CPT Pedrosa, SFC Merely Maynard, and unknown CID.

hand to call the camp. I saw that I was bleeding from my left forearm and the blood was dripping on the ground. I swore to myself that this was the last of my blood that I would ever leave on the ground in Vietnam and took the handset with my right hand and called in the contact. I gave them our coordinates and requested artillery fire from the two ARVN 105's. I wanted to get some shelling started on the enemy's position. I also requested a medevac, as I noticed a couple of wounded CIDs being worked on by the CID medics.

We continued to fire across the trail as we regrouped. We then began to move very carefully west through the jungle toward the rubber plantation because the artillery salvos were now arriving and blowing up everything on the south side of the trail.

A medevac was on the way when we reached the edge of the jungle. I checked on Maynard again. The wound was to the web of his hand between the thumb and index finger, probably a pellet from the Chicom claymore. I bandaged his hand and put a bandage on the wound on my left forearm, also probably from a pellet from the claymore. I was lucky because I had been hit in the upper part of my left forearm, which was across my left side resting on the claymore bag where I carried extra ammo. If my arm had not been there, the claymore pellet would have gone into my abdomen and caused a lot of internal damage.

I tried to get Maynard to leave on the medevac but he refused. I should have gotten on the medevac myself but I did not want to leave Maynard alone. He was still disorientated from the explosion of the claymores, and if the enemy came after us, he was in no shape to fight. Nor did I relish the prospect of going to a field hospital somewhere and getting stuck there overnight, so we both stayed with the operation. The CID who had been walking in front of Maynard was wounded; the CID who was directly behind my radio man was KIA; a couple of CIDs further back were seriously wounded and needed to be medevac'd. The chopper came in and we loaded on the casualties.

We were just inside the edge of the rubber trees and were about to start heading toward the camp when a helicopter with the B-Team lieutenant colonel on board flew overhead. I was on the radio with him and he ordered us to, "Go back into the jungle after the bad guys and get back into the fight."

Author with wounded left arm in February 1969.

I responded that we had, "Two Whiskey-India-Alpha-Alphas" (Two Wounded in Action Americans—Maynard and me) and numerous CIDs with minor wounds. I added that, "We are spent and out of ammo."

But he didn't care. His response was, "Get back into the jungle and engage the enemy!"

I again explained, "We are out of ammo and have nothing left to fight with."

That must have really pissed him off because he gave me a direct order for the third time to, "Get back into the jungle."

I told him, "I am in charge of this operation and we are going back to camp. If you want to be in charge of the operation, you can land and relieve me of my command."

He might have been intending to do that when the helicopter started to receive automatic weapons fire from inside the jungle. The chopper with the B-Team lieutenant colonel on board went from hovering approximately 200 feet above us to being a small speck in the sky in a matter of seconds.

"Over and out, sir."

I didn't hear from him again. We resumed walking back to camp and arrived about two hours later.

A month later the same lieutenant colonel came to our camp at Loc Ninh and presented Maynard and me with Purple Hearts for the wounds we had received on February 15. While pinning the medals on us he stated, "I am proud of you men."

My response was, "No sir we f***ed up."

"I am proud of you because you were out mixing it up with the enemy," he said.

I repeated myself. "No sir we f***ed up."

Which we had. We were lazy. We were walking on a trail that we shouldn't have been on, and had got hit.

———————

That was the last time I ever let an operation walk on a trail again. Once on a later mission, the CIDs had started to do so while coming back from a 'Yard village to the west of camp. When I tried to get them to spread out they said, "No sweat *Bac Si*, no VC."

They refused to listen to me so I fired two magazines into the air and told them, "*Beaucoup* VC now!"

They got off the trail and into formation and we made it back to camp with no further problems.

CHAPTER **22**

AMBUSH AT AN LOC

<hr />

S FC ANDEE CHAPMAN AND I were going to run a multiple-company
operation south of our camp in the B-Team AO north of An Loc. American Bell UH-1 Iroquois helicopters (Hueys) came and picked up the two
of us and our CIDG troops at the A-331 airstrip. We inserted onto a big
grassy field in the middle of the jungle, 10 klicks northeast of An Loc. Usually a Huey can carry only six or seven Americans due to weight restrictions,
but we didn't have that restriction, as our people weighed only about 100
pounds each. This was my first combat helicopter insertion in Vietnam.

As we touched down on the landing zone the troops on my bird were

SFC Andee Chapman in the communications bunker.

very hesitant to get off, so I stood in the middle of the passenger bay and pushed them out the door. I wanted to get that Huey out of there. I also wanted to get some fire power on the ground in case there were any bad guys lurking nearby. Several of the CIDs tumbled out in a heap, but once on the ground they took off like scared rabbits to the edge of the clearing and set up a defensive position. The other choppers now touched down and troops were disembarking okay and running over to join up with us. It was a good thing that we did not encounter any initial resistance. If that had happened, there was no way we could have gotten any more of the CIDs off the choppers, and those of us already on the ground would have been sitting ducks.

We were out for a five-day reconnaissance-in-force operation in the area, as Intel had reports of a major NVA movement and build up. Recon-in-force involves engaging the enemy, causing it to reveal its strength and deployment, but not necessarily to defeat it in a battle. The purpose is primarily to gather information.

We were told the NVA had bypassed Loc Ninh as it moved deeper into South Vietnam, and was preparing to hit An Loc. Our mission was to see if we could locate any of them and if so, to identify their units and troop-strength. An Loc, also called Quan Loi, had a good-sized American base that housed our B-Team as well as regular US Army troops and some heavy-duty artillery (175mm) that could reach all the way to our camp's AO. If we did find any major NVA build up, the information would be passed up the chain of command and would probably lead to a major US or ARVN operation to engage them.

On the second day out, we jumped a couple of bad guys which led to a small skirmish but nothing major. We searched the area but did not find any bodies and figured they had run off into the jungle.

On the fourth day we stopped to rest and eat lunch at the southern edge of a very large open area, nearly the size of 10 football fields. The troops finished their meal and then we packed up and moved to the east along the southern edge of the field while keeping under cover just inside the tree line. At the end of the field we were ambushed by maybe seven bad guys who were hiding behind a couple of small knolls, some trees, and fallen logs. All kinds of hell broke out as the enemy was firing their AK-47's right at us and our troops were firing back.

Chapman and I were close to the point of attack. We dropped down behind a couple of mounds of dirt about two feet high and tried to figure out what was going on. I got off a couple of mags and noticed that one of our troops was down. He was in front of and to the left of us, maybe 10 yards away. The poor guy was wounded, unable to move, and out in the open. If he stayed there, the NVA would surely finish him off.

Chapman yelled at me, "Go get him *Bac Si*. I'll cover you."

I yelled back, "Why don't you go get him and I'll cover you?"

"Because you're the *Bac Si*!" was his response.

This whole time we were still exchanging fire with the bad guys who were approximately 40 yards in front of us. I must have said something like, "F*** you Chapman," more than a few times.

He again said, "Go on, I got you covered!" and shot up the area in front of us with his M-16 on full-auto.

I ran in a low crouching position to the wounded CID and dragged him back five feet so that he was behind a small mound of dirt, and began to fire in the direction of the enemy. The whole time Chapman was shooting at everything in front of us—he had my back and the CID was rescued. While still firing and half-lying on top of the CID, I noticed that he had been shot through the left thigh.

Just then our troops rallied and charged our attackers. They were always very brave when they had superior numbers—which in this case was almost ten to one. The bad guys *didi mau'd* off into the bush, and the CIDs chased them awhile then re-formed around the site of the ambush. The CIDs said that the VC must be on a suicide mission because they were screaming at us about how they were pissed because we had killed some of their friends a couple of days ago.

Something was wrong. It didn't make any sense for a squad of seven to try to ambush a company-sized force, even if you allowed for the revenge factor.

One of the CID medics came over and helped me bandage the wounded man's thigh. We put the leg in a splint, gave him a shot of morphine for pain, and got an IV going. Meanwhile, Chapman and I were trying to figure out what to do next. We had a couple other CIDs with minor wounds. They would be fine but the one who was shot through the thigh was going to need a medevac to get him out of there.

Fortunately we had the big field to the north so it would not be a problem getting the chopper in, but we wanted to make sure the landing area was safe. We sent out a couple of platoons to move around the edge of the field and secure it on the north and west sides. But they didn't get very far. They stopped when they were no more than 75 yards from us; they were very scared. That's when we realized that a main body of NVA had set up on the north end of the field and were protected by the jungle. They were waiting for us to go out into the middle of the open field so they could spring a big-time ambush and maybe shoot down a chopper for good measure. That must have been their plan all along. Harass us with a squad, inflict some casualties and cause confusion, then lure us into the open field where they could hit us with full force. They would easily pick us off and wipe us out.

We got everyone set up in a defensive perimeter and radioed in our situation. We said we had a WIA that needed to be medevac'd and were potentially facing a couple hundred enemy across the way who were ready to jump us.

It was our good fortune that the Air Force had a couple of fast movers (jets) about 10 minutes from our location. The FAC (Forward Air Controller) spotter plane flying over the area got in touch with us. We told him the bad guys were at the north end of the field inside the tree line and we were on the south end. We popped colored smoke so he could identify our location. We wanted to have the jets make their runs east to west to be sure nothing short or long was dropped on us. That was "rule one" when calling in air strikes—never call them in over your position. The FAC plane marked the north end of the field with smoke and gave the okay for the jets to come in.

They came roaring in from our right and flew over the north end of the field above the jungle across from us. They dropped little black canisters which exploded into huge fire balls when they hit. Napalm. The whole wood line lit up with bright orange flames that climbed 50 feet into the air. Nothing could have survived the heat and fire. The bad guys literally were toast. We sent a platoon across the field to check things out and to secure the area. All that was left after the air strike was smoldering ashes. The jungle had been incinerated along with anyone who was there waiting to ambush us.

The north side of the field was now secured so we called in a medevac chopper to pick up the wounded CID. I advised him of our location and situation, and told him, "We need the wounded to be taken to the Special Forces Hospital at the C-Team at Bien Hoa."

I knew that they would normally drop him off at an ARVN facility and not an American hospital. But since he still had a good strong pulse in his ankle, indicating no serious artery damage, the leg could be operated on, set, and saved. I did not trust the doctors at an ARVN hospital to do that.

The medevac radioed and asked us to identify ourselves. I popped a smoke grenade and he identified the color and the chopper came in for a landing. We loaded the wounded CID onboard and I yelled over the noise of the rotating helicopter blades to the pilot, "Take him to the Special Forces Hospital at Bien Hoa!" and he nodded in agreement.

When the medevac left, SFC Chapman, a large black man, said to me, "You know *Bac Si*, you've got a black man's heart." I wasn't sure exactly what he meant until years later, but I always took it as a great compliment.

After we got back to camp and were debriefed I was told that I was going to be put in for a medal for what I did, maybe even a Silver Star. Chapman was going to be put in for a medal also. On our recon-in-force operation not only did we find and verify the buildup of a large NVA element, but through the use of superior American air power we were able to put a significant hurt on them.

A couple of months later the wounded CID came back to camp on crutches and on one leg. I guess the medevac got diverted and had ended up in an ARVN hospital after all. They probably chopped off his leg without ever trying to save it.

I don't know if Chapman got a medal for his actions. I know that I never did.

CHAPTER 23

RECON

———————————————

THE LATEST B-TEAM DIRECTIVE for our A-Team was to have one multi-company and one reconnaissance operation in the field at all times. The multi-company operations were to be five-day missions and the recon operations were to be three-day missions.

SFC Andee Chapman and I were on a three-day recon patrol with an objective of scouting an area to the south of Loc Ninh for possible enemy movement. The patrol was made up of 30 CIDs combined from the two recon platoons, primarily composed of Vietnamese and Montagnard troops. On a three-day recon patrol you did not have to carry as many rations as you would on a five-day, multi-company operation. Because your backpack was not quite as heavy, you could walk much faster through the woods even while carrying the same amount of ammo.

We had proceeded south from the camp and through the rubber plantation and entered the bush. The area was very hilly but not particularly thick with vegetation. There were numerous paths and open areas. It looked like it had been hit with a couple of Arc Light (B-52) bombing runs and also sprayed by Agent Orange some time previously, so moving through the area was fairly easy.

We came upon an abandoned NVA bunker complex that appeared to have taken a direct hit from a B-52 strike. The B-52's would fly over areas of reported enemy activity and drop 500- or 750-pound bombs on the target zone. Each plane had an external payload of up to 24 bombs, and the noise of them detonating from five or even 10 miles away was deafening. Each explosion would leave a crater nearly 15 feet in diameter and six to seven feet deep in the middle.

As we moved through the destroyed NVA bunker complex, every 30 feet there would be another crater of the same size and then another. Anyone or anything taking a direct hit from one of these strikes would not stand a chance. I had never seen an area that had actually been hit by a B-52 strike before, though I had seen some craters this big. We could tell that there was nothing left here. The few bunkers that were still identifiable were caved in as if they had been crushed. Others were just blown apart. I could tell the strike had been fairly recent because the ground was very soft, like it had been freshly tilled. We did not come across any bodies—only some shredded pieces of webbing and damaged equipment.

It looked like the B-52's had dropped their big bombs right up Charlie's ass and tore him a new one. We radioed in our BDA (Bomb Damage Assessment) and moved further to the southwest.

On the second day we stopped to rest on the top of a large hill that had a bomb crater right in the middle of it. We were approximately 50 feet away from the major path we'd been following that ran east-west. I sat on the edge of the crater with my feet in it. The sides gently sloped to the bottom and it felt like a nice comfortable chair. All of a sudden we heard chopping noises in the distance. Everybody crouched down and got quiet. The troops whispered to Andee and me, "VC, VC!"

The chopping noise became much clearer now and there was a lot of it. Carefully, we crawled in that direction to determine exactly what was causing it. I could not see anything, but a couple of CIDs said that some VC were chopping logs to build a bunker complex on the north side of the next hill, about one klick to our west. Of course, it was "*Beaucoup VC*"—that's all we could ever get from the CIDs. But based on the amount of chopping and the 20 or 30 NVA that were now visible on the south side of the hill, we estimated that it was at least a company-size encampment. A full-strength NVA company ranged from 125 to 250 soldiers, and we figured this group was at least 200. Our patrol had 30 troops plus Andee and myself.

In this area, the NVA would always build their complexes on the north side of a hill, as they were leery of the artillery at An Loc. A complex on the south side of a hill would be extremely vulnerable to artillery fire from the south, but it was a much more difficult shot for the big guns if the complex was situated on a northern slope. I would do the same if I were in their position. But even though it was a difficult shot, it was not an impossible one.

Andee got on the radio and let the camp know our position and situation. They got us hooked up with the 175mm US artillery at An Loc, and Andee directed the shelling onto the backside of that next hill. Once he had walked the artillery onto the NVA's position, he had them fire for effect. The idea was to fire away and blow up the entire area. The incoming volleys blasted the hillside for another five minutes until all we could see was smoke and dust. We called off the artillery, as they had done their job, and told them we would check out the area and give them a body count.

How they loved body counts. Most of the time the artillery would fire at pre-determined targets where Intelligence suspected enemy activity, but unless someone checked out the area later, they would never know how effective their efforts had been. But if they had a real live target and could find out that they had blown up some bad guys, they were elated.

Of course, we weren't too excited about going over to the next hill and checking out the area since we didn't know how many enemy might be left. We felt that we were already lucky enough that they hadn't spotted us. The NVA had to suspect that someone was observing them, someone must have called the artillery directly on top of their heads. If any had survived they would surely be on the lookout for us.

Operation preparing to move out.

We sat down in our position for a couple of minutes and kept quiet to see what might happen. Hell, if they still had a couple hundred and we were only 30, then advantage NVA. We couldn't know for sure how many had survived but the odds were that they out-numbered us at least three or four to one. Not good odds. So we sat tight.

One of the older CIDs had fought with the Viet Minh against the French. He wasn't a Communist, but he hated the French and all their colonial puppets as much as he loved the Americans. A lot of times on patrol he would wear his old Viet Minh pith helmet, and to look at him— fiftyish, Vietnamese, faded fatigues, pith helmet, wispy mustache—he looked like an old Viet Minh, which he was.

Unexpectedly, we heard movement coming our way from the direction of the hillside that had just been had shelled. *Shit!* Now they were coming after us and we had no chance if they discovered us. Our options were to run like hell out of there or to hide, and hiding was not an option if they were really trying to find us. We could see them moving off the other hill and heading toward us while following the east-west trail that went right by our position. There was a whole bunch of them too. For once it was time for me to say, "*Beaucoup VC!*"

I spotted 20 to 30 NVA approaching us, with many more behind them. We were about to bolt when we realized that they were not looking for us but simply moving *en masse* to another location. They were talking amongst themselves and not proceeding in any type of combat formation.

Holy crap! They were right on us and it was too late to split and run. The old CID with the Viet Minh pith helmet put down his weapon and walked over to the trail while the rest of us hid. Andee and I were in the B-52 crater with our heads down and out of sight. We could hear the old CID greeting and talking to the NVA troops as they walked along the trail only 50 feet away from us. I guess that they thought he was just a local VC and did not pay much attention to him. The NVA troops kept on going as if they were soldiers following orders to move to a new location. They did not even bother to check out the hilltop and the crater where we were hidden.

Around 200 of them marched by. A good-sized company. It was fortunate for Andee and me that the B-52 crater was there to hide in. While our CID troops were ragged-looking enough to pass as local VC, if the NVA had spotted the two of us—Andee, a 6-foot tall black man, and my-

self, a 5:11 white guy with blond hair—we would definitely be identified
as the enemy and the end results would have been a whole lot different.

Once the NVA company had moved a ways past us the old CID came
back chuckling. He said he was out there greeting the enemy as they walked
by, asking how they were and what had happened. Once we were sure there
were no more coming our way from the blown up hillside, we got the hell
out of there and headed north to the rubber trees and back to camp. If any
of the NVA had put it together that there was an old Viet Minh talking to
them as they were leaving their bunker area that had been hit by very accurate artillery fire, and that someone had to have called in that artillery, they
might have wondered who the old guy was and what he was doing there.

For all I know they did figure it out and sent someone back to question
him. It didn't matter though because by that time we were far from the
area. There were too many bad guys for us to handle. But we had done
our job as a recon platoon—we found the enemy and even put some artillery down their throats, while reporting on their strength and new movements. I believe that some American troops were sent in after them, as the
NVA were only about four miles north of An Loc, their likely next target.

———————

About two miles south of Loc Ninh on Highway 13, the RFPF had a small
contingent in a hamlet with a name you could not pronounce. I had never
been there, as it was never an objective in any of my operations in the field.
There was no reported VC activity in its vicinity, and because of that, our
operations didn't bother with it since we had other hot spots that the Intelligence people wanted us to check out. We employed a numbering system
for the local villages around Loc Ninh, i.e., 1 through 10, because we could
not pronounce their real names. This particular hamlet was not even included on the list, or if it was no one remembered what its number was.

But then the little RFPF contingent was hit a couple nights in a row.
They reported that they were receiving incoming fire from RPGs, mortars,
and small arms fire from "*beaucoup* VC." We could not determine what
kind of force was attacking them. It could have been a small group of five
or six local VC harassing them, or it could have been a larger group of
NVA. The NVA would sometimes hit smaller targets with their new recruits to give them some combat experience before engaging larger Amer-

ican or South Vietnamese Army units. Their well-trained, hardcore troops would only be used for those assaults with the objective of wiping out our position.

I was sent out on a three-day recon operation with about 30 CIDs, to go scout the area around the RFPF compound to see if we could determine the strength of the attacking force and its location. The little hamlet was at the southernmost extent of the rubber plantation. Our best guess was that the bad guys were moving in from the east to hit the compound, so that's where we hiked to. Along the way there would be a grove of rubber trees for about 100 feet, then there would be regular trees and the normal creeping vines and high weeds. It looked like a long time ago the owners had tried to extend the rubber plantation by planting more trees, but never quite finished the job.

The first day's hike was uneventful. We set up in our overnight position in a grove of trees less than a mile east of the hamlet and about 200 feet north of the main east-west trail that led directly into it. The sky was overcast and it was so dark you could barely see your hand in front of your face.

Everything was quiet until about midnight, when we were awakened by the sound of explosions coming from the direction of the RPFP compound. The bad guys were definitely firing RPGs and mortars at them. We could actually see the bright but faint flashes of light in the sky when the rounds detonated. We radioed into our camp and gave them the situation—"A good size group of probably NVA are mortaring and firing RPGs at the RFPFs. We don't see them so they must be attacking from the western side of the hamlet." There was nothing more for us to do, as it was too dark to move and the NVA probably outnumbered us. The assault only lasted about 15 minutes, then all was silent and quiet again.

We figured that the NVA had moved in from the west side of the hamlet along the east-west trail because we didn't see them. This meant we could eliminate the possibility of their being near us on the eastern side. That's what we thought anyway, for about 20 minutes, until the CIDs all started to become agitated. Because it was so dark they could now see lights coming down the trail from the direction of the RFPF compound. They were headed directly toward us. Everyone got down and stayed real quiet as approximately 100 NVA troops, with about every fifth one holding a flash light, walked along the trail that was only 200 feet to our south. The bad guys were passing right in front of us. They proceeded down the trail worry free, probably talking amongst themselves about the attack, while we were hiding for our lives.

The east-west trail was on the maps that we carried. So once the enemy was past our location and out of earshot we again radioed in and gave the grid for a fire mission by the 105's in camp. We estimated how far the NVA would have walked in the five or so minutes it took to get the howitzers going, and the big guns blasted the entire area with everything they had.

Surprise Charlie! We found you. And even though we could not engage you in a firefight because there were too few of us and too many of you, we knew where you were coming from and going to and hopefully hit you with the artillery fire we called in on your ass.

———————————

We had been reconning in the jungle east of Loc Ninh and south of highway 14. It was a miserable patrol, hacking our way through thick underbrush and vines while a light rain fell most of the time. The jungle was damp and steamy and we were all somewhat drenched. A poncho would keep the mist off your shoulders and torso but from the knees down you were just wet and soggy. At night, though, the poncho at least kept the drizzling rain off while you tried to sleep in your hammock.

On day two we turned a little north and planned to approach Village 10 from the southern jungle side, so we would not be detected. Village 10 was at the southern boundary of the rubber plantation that ran east along the old highway 14. We were almost there when the CIDs up front stopped and crouched down and got real quiet. The whole operation went quiet.

At the edge of the jungle was what looked to be a football-field sized hayfield that lay between rows of rubber trees and the village. The CIDs were at the point where the jungle ended and the hayfield began when they all opened up. Some VC were on the opposite side of the field apparently on guard duty, and who knows who spotted who first or fired first. But the CIDs were now all blasting away. By the time I made it to the edge of the jungle, about half of the CIDs had already crossed the hayfield and were standing on the other side. It wasn't that I was that slow. It's just that you can't move too fast through the last few feet of jungle.

There had been only two or three VC on the other side but they were long gone, having run off through the rubber trees in the direction of Village 10. They had been holed up in an approximately eight-foot by eight-foot open-sided, thatched roof structure supported by four ten-foot tall poles. It was filled with hay and it sure seemed like a nice cozy place to be if you wanted to avoid the drizzling rain. There was no sign that any of the VC had been hit, and there was no chance of us catching up with them. It looked like our surprise visit to Village 10 had been compromised. If any bad guys had been hiding in the village they would have been warned and would have fled by now. But I decided we ought to go there and check it out anyway.

But first we had to deal with all this hay. The CIDs were standing around the structure and my thoughts were, "I wonder if the bad guys have some type of arms cache hidden under it." In our training we had been told that the VC hid their extra ammo, guns, and rockets in caches so they would be available when they needed them. After all, all of their munitions had to be transported from North Vietnam down through Laos and Cambodia into South Vietnam. I had never been on an operation that had found a cache but I knew of several others that had. When that happened, the troops would then bring everything back to the camp where it would be destroyed. This haystack was dry and seemed to be a logical hiding place.

I told the interpreter "Let's get someone to check out the hay to see if they have anything hidden there."

He said, "No, no *Bac Si,* maybe VC booby trap."

That also sounded logical. Why take a chance of getting blown up? So as we moved away from the haystack and started for the village a couple of CIDs lit it on fire. It burned real bright behind us, crackling with flames that reached the thatched roof, destroying the structure and all the hay in it. But there were no secondary explosions from any ammo cooking off from the fire and heat. I guess the VC were just using the little structure to stay dry while on guard duty.

We swept Village 10 but naturally there was nothing but old women and children who kept saying, "No VC here." We left the village to continue our patrol, with all of us realizing that the enemy now knew where we were. We would have to be super careful and on guard until we reached the camp.

CHAPTER **24**

INCOMING AT AN LOC

S FC ANDEE CHAPMAN AND I were on another multi-company helicopter insertion in the B-Team AO east of An Loc. Andee and I had
become regular partners on operations by now.

Intelligence had it that there were several battalions of NVA regulars
building up in the area for an assault on An Loc, which had been taking
incoming every night from 122mm rocket attacks. The rockets were not
effectively directed at anything, but were nonetheless hitting the B-Team
and the American base. To fire a 122mm rocket at a large target like An
Loc, you did not need to be an excellent shot. All you needed was to know
the general direction and the approximate distance. Then prop up the
rocket and fire it in the direction of An Loc and *voila*—bulls-eye. Rocket
science 101.

Our mission was to locate and identify any of the NVA regulars in the
area. We were also to see if we could track down the bad guys shooting
those rockets at An Loc.

The helicopter insertion went well. We encountered no hostiles on
the ground and moved quickly out of the area, as the noise of the choppers
was sure to draw attention to our arrival. If there were a lot of NVA regulars
around we wanted to find them and not have them find us. The first day
was uneventful. We spent it breaking through the bush and not observing
much of anything. All day long however, the CIDs were very nervous and
edgy. It seemed they could sense that there were a lot of bad guys around.

We stopped for the night in the general area where the B-Team believed the rocket fire was coming from. Everyone was resting when around
10 o'clock we heard the 122mm rockets being launched one at a time.

At left, SGT Tom Reisinger, medic, ready to go on patrol with CO Captain Harry Zimmerman.

They made a loud whooshing sound when taking off and approximately 20 seconds later you could hear them splash (explode) at An Loc.

The rockets were being fired about a klick away from us. Chapman radioed in to the B-Team and told them we had discovered where the rocket attacks were originating. He provided them with the coordinates and requested artillery fire. There must not have been many bad guys involved since they were only launching one rocket every three or four minutes or so.

There was a problem with getting the US artillery involved, as they needed permission from the Vietnamese District Chief to fire if there was no direct contact with the enemy. Andee kept yelling at them on the radio that we had located the bad guys, and "they are rocketing you right now and you need to start shooting the big 175's," but nothing happened. Finally, I was so frustrated and pissed that I got on the radio and started calling out the shots like we did when we were calling in our own artillery.

Whenever a rocket was launched, I would say, "Shot out!" then count off 20 seconds and announce "Splash!" Right after I said "Splash" we could hear the rocket exploding at An Loc. I did this for four consecutive firings before someone there came to their senses and got the US guns going.

Chapman directed the artillery, which sounded like it was hitting all over the area that the rockets were being fired from. Soon the rocketing ceased. A direct hit by us. We were now concerned because we knew that the guys who fired the rockets would be moving out of the area due to the artillery barrage, and we didn't know which way they would be headed. We were also concerned because we didn't know if the bad guys' friends would be arriving to assist the rocket guys, and had no idea where they would be coming from.

After waiting for a couple of hours with nothing happening, we were certain that the NVA had moved out of the area and not toward us. After remaining awake and alert for so long, I finally settled down to get some sleep.

While on a mission, we maintained radio contact with the camp at all times and would inform them of our position every time we stopped to rest for the night. Even though we were in communication with the camp, as long as we patrolled in the assigned area and carried out our objectives, we were in charge of our own operation. We decided where we were going and when. The camp did not micromanage things.

The following morning Chapman and I conferred to determine our next move.

The 122mm rocket attack from last night had come from a location just north of us, and was directed at the B-Team which was to the west of us. It would not be smart for the enemy to launch rockets from their encampment. In order to avoid detection and not invite an attack on the main force, the rocket crews would have set up closer to their target. We figured they slipped in from the east, and once the artillery started falling on them had scrambled back to the encampment. We decided not to go to where the rocket fire had been coming from since there was probably nothing there. Instead we would head east a couple of klicks and then turn north to see if we could find any bad guys.

We moved out and walked for two klicks, stopped for a rest, and then proceeded north. The area was slightly higher in elevation and very lush, with tall trees and not much underbrush; it reminded me of a typical forest in northern Michigan. And the weather was very hot. The ground all around was pockmarked by small craters approximately two feet deep.

Grass had grown back into them, leading me to think they were most likely the result of artillery fire or aerial bombs from years ago.

Suddenly, small arms fire broke out from the lead platoon of the formation. The CIDs were moving up, firing their weapons, and giving chase. We had jumped some bad guys—a small squad of NVA. The shooting had died down by the time I arrived at the front and I saw five or six CIDs standing around a small depression with their M-16's leveled and pointing down. They were all talking and yelling at once and from their looks were ready to fire. I ran up and looked down.

A young female NVA Vietnamese was lying on her back, apparently wounded, with an expression of utter fear on her face. Based on what I had seen the CIDs do previously, I practically dove into the depression and covered her with my body before they could execute her.

They were now yelling at me, "VC *Bac Si*, VC *Bac Si!*" and I was yelling back at them "*Didi, didi me ngu!*" meaning essentially, "Go, go you mother****ers."

They kept on yelling and I yelled "*Bac Si caca dau* (kill) you if you not *didi mau.*"

One of the CID medics came up and I motioned him into the depression beside me. And then some of the other CIDs came over along with the LLDB and Chapman. Those who had been standing around and pointing their weapons at me and the female NVA backed off. Once they did so the CID medic and I began to examine her.

Her eyes were wide as saucers. She was totally terrified at the commotion surrounding her and by the rifles aimed at her; she must have realized she was wounded and wondered why an American was now lying half on top of her. She had been hit in the right wrist and in the butt. The CID medic and I bandaged and splinted the wrist, bandaged her bottom, got an IV started, and gave her a shot of morphine for pain. While I was doing this Chapman was on the radio requesting a medevac.

We later learned she was an NVA nurse and was not even carrying a weapon when the squad she was with encountered our troops. The rest of her friends got away but she was wounded and could not run. The chopper arrived and landed in a little clearing. We loaded her on and away she went. We had taken a prisoner and our Intelligence people would try to find out what unit she was with and anything else she knew.

Score one for our side.

We rested then moved east to see what else we could turn up. It was now the middle of day two of our five-day operation and we knew there were some active NVA in the area, and not the usual ragtag local VC. The CIDs were getting really spooked at the idea of going against hardcore NVA units. But the remainder of the day was uneventful as we cautiously made our way through the bush and eventually stopped to settle in for the night.

The first thing the next day we talked to the powers-that-be. They wanted us to check out an area still further east of us, as they had received reports of movements by multiple NVA battalions. We set out in the morning and after walking for a couple of hours, the CIDs totally freaked out. We had stopped for a mid-morning break but when we got ready to move out they would not go any further. All they could say was, *"Beaucoup* VC, *beaucoup* VC!"* and point in the direction we were supposed to go.

Chapman radioed in and told the camp what was happening, but we again received direct orders from the B-Team. We were to proceed to the east. Chapman talked to the CIDs but they continued to balk. They said they were getting out of here. We were at a standoff. Chapman and I refused to go back, and the troops refused to go any further. They were turning around no matter what.

We radioed in again and were told to stand our ground and get them moving to the east. But the CIDs and the LLDB had slipped away and were headed west in the direction of An Loc; even our two radio operators had dropped the units they were carrying and fled. The standoff had ended. Chapman and I stood our ground and the troops, with the exception of Nick, our interpreter, took off.

Chapman got on the radio and asked the B-Team "What the hell do we do now?"

It was just SFC Andee Chapman, Nick, me, and two radios in the middle of the jungle with multiple NVA battalions all around on the move and looking for us.

What a lovely spot to be in!

Andee had been in Vietnam before, serving in recon with the 173rd Airborne; Nick had been an interpreter at Loc Ninh for about six years; and I had been in-country for a while now. I wasn't a rookie so I knew we could maneuver through the bush okay, but if we met up with even a squad of NVA, much less a battalion on the move, we would be decimated. The B-Team had taken over our operation and gotten us into this mess—and it was the B-Team that arranged an extraction for us. They sent up a Huey to get us out, along with a Loach (Light Observation Helicopter). Two Cobra gunships were also coming our way to cover us if needed.

We were in radio contact with the Huey. The pilot was scouting around for a clearing big enough for a suitable LZ, but could not find anything except a small open area where maybe the Loach could land. The Loach was a very small chopper that normally would zigzag at low altitude during an air operation to draw fire so that the Cobras could then locate the enemy and attack them. There wasn't enough room in the back of a Loach for two Americans and an interpreter plus two radios.

The Huey was giving us directions to the small open area and we were slowly and cautiously heading that way through the brush. The Loach and the two Cobra gunships came up on the radio and said they had spotted our CIDs moving very fast to the west. The Cobra pilots asked us, "Do you want us to open up and waste them?"

We said, "No, no—don't fire!"

They replied, "Roger that; do not fire on the bug outs." It would have served the little bastards right though if they had.

We finally made it to the clearing but it was small and not big enough for a full-sized Huey to set down. Keeping to the edge in the brush we popped a smoke grenade and the Loach identified the color. We acknowledged and the Loach approached for a landing. After it touched down Nick got into the back along with the two radios. Then Chapman climbed in and was lying on top of Nick. There was no room for me inside the aircraft so I stepped up onto the right landing skid, got hold of a metal handle on the door frame, and waved the pilot to go.

Chapman grabbed on to me and as overloaded as the Loach was, it still managed to take off. Unbeknownst to us, our orders had been changed. The LLDB at the B-Team wanted us to rejoin the CIDs and our LLDB associate, who was actually in charge of the operation.

It didn't take long to find them and the Loach landed on a small trail they were walking on. With the two sister Cobra gunships overhead providing cover if needed, I hopped off the skid and then Chapman and Nick climbed out. We saluted and waved to the two-man Loach crew and hurried down the trail to rejoin our troops just ahead of us. Our orders were to link up with them and go along with them to wherever they were going. And they were headed straight to An Loc by the shortest means possible!

The "official" mission of Special Forces in Vietnam was as advisors to the LLDB—the Vietnamese Special Forces. On every operation we had an LLDB counterpart with us who was supposedly in charge, but often could not be found when there was any type of contact with the enemy. Our role "officially" was to coordinate air support and call in artillery strikes, though in reality we were directing the troops in any situation that occurred once the shooting started. I supposed there had been some kind of diplomatic brouhaha at the B-Team between our commander and the LLDB commander, and that's why we were ordered to accompany the CIDs and the LLDB.

So Chapman, Nick, and I now joined the march toward An Loc and were eventually walking down the middle of a wide two-track road. A perfect place for an ambush by the bad guys. It was late in the afternoon and we were about a half hour out of An Loc when up in the front of the formation there was some sort of commotion.

A company of US Army troops was preparing to set up an ambush on the trail for the night. They were not yet in place when they spotted us approaching. Fortunately, the American soldiers were seasoned troops and saw that our guys were carrying M-16's and had on camo jungle fatigues. The CIDs did not look like VC or NVA, and so the Americans did not open fire. The CIDs were all smiling and waving at the Americans as we walked past them.

A lieutenant came running up to Chapman and me and said something like, "What the F*** are you doing walking through my F***ing ambush site? Don't you know we could have F***ed you up?"

Chapman and I replied, "Sorry sir, but we're just 'advisors' here and we advised them not to do this. We're only along for the ride."

The lieutenant went back to his troops while cursing to himself. His ambush site had been compromised by our walking through it and by the interactions between the CIDs and the GI's. Hopefully he moved his ambush to a different location.

Actually, we were very lucky. In another hour or so the company would have been dug in to its ambush position along the road and might not have readily recognized the CIDs as a friendly force. In that case, they could have wiped us out.

It was right at dusk when we entered the B-Team compound at An Loc. We settled in for the night and the next day were choppered back to Loc Ninh. I never heard anything further regarding the reason Chapman, Nick, and I had been ordered to rejoin the troops.

A month or so later, Chief visited us for some kind of inspection at our camp. Chief (his nickname) was a chief warrant officer who had been attached to our team when I first arrived at Loc Ninh. When he was there we had a baby spider monkey, a kitten, and a baby weasel that we raised together. They were kept in a big cage and they ate and slept together and became friends. The little monkey would sleep with one of his arms around the weasel or the kitten. When Chief left, he took Willy the Weasel with him to Nha Trang. He was telling me a story of how a German shepherd once tried to attack Willy the Weasel, who responded by ripping out the dog's neck.

Then he told me some news about the NVA nurse that we had captured. The South Vietnamese interrogated all the prisoners we took, and passed on whatever information they obtained to their American counterparts. Chief said that in the process of questioning the NVA nurse, one of the Vietnamese interrogators tore off her right hand, the one that had been shot and which I had bandaged and splinted. She was still alive but was missing her right hand now.

I drank a whole lot of beer and passed out on my bunk that night after hearing that story.

CHAPTER 25

TEAM WITH A TANK

Special Forces camp A-331 at Loc Ninh had a distinction that no other Special Forces A-Team in Vietnam had. We had a tank! An M-48 tank sitting on the north wall of our defensive berm. It wasn't operational but there it was, with its big 90mm gun pointing out over the berm, aimed at the rubber plantation 100 yards away. It looked very impressive. A tank was definitely not standard Army issue for an A-Team. In fact, not a single one of us even knew how to operate it.

This is how it came to be ours. The 11th Cav was running an operation in our AO and the M-48 hit a mine. I had never seen or heard of anti-personnel or anti-tank mines being used by the NVA anywhere around us,

M-48 Tank, visible in the background at the berm.

but apparently they had them, and had used them to try to stop the 11th Cav. The M-48 was so well built that none of the soldiers riding inside were injured when it struck the mine, but it did knock out the engine, the drive train, and the operating system. Everything else remained intact—the body, the 90mm gun, and the interior. Because the tank was so severely damaged, the 11th Cav guys were going to strip it then take it off somewhere and blow it up.

Our CO and Top were pretty close to the 11th Cav officers, as they operated in our AO so often, so they made a deal. We would trade a 10-kilowatt generator for the tank if the 11th Cav would drag it into camp and place it on the berm. All of the electricity for the camp was from a couple of 20-kilowatt generators, one of which was always running while the other was being refueled or maintained. Nobody had any idea where the 10K generator had come from—it wasn't even on our property record. After the deal was made, the tank was brought in and set up at the berm on the north side of the camp. We were now the proud owners of an M-48 tank.

The weapons guys on the team and I checked it out. You couldn't keep me away from our new toy. It was so cool. We mounted a 50-caliber machine gun on top of it. It looked real impressive. Then we started to explore the interior. With no engine there was no power for any of the systems, but we figured out how to manually crank the 90mm gun up and down and from side to side. The weapons guys also figured out how to load a shell into the breach, and found where the trigger was. We had a few shells on hand that the 11th Cav gave us, but we were afraid to fire the big gun. What if the barrel or the firing mechanism was damaged and blew up?

The weapons guys knew all about weapons, except how to safely fire the 90mm gun. They thought that they had done their share and it was now my turn to contribute to our self-appointed tank team project.

I said, "The Army has a manual for everything, and I do mean everything, so they must have a manual for an M-48 Tank." We didn't know if we could actually get a manual or if someone would review the request and question it. I thought it was worth a try.

The weapons guys agreed and it became my responsibility to order the manual. I sent out a request for an M-48 manual on our daily radio situation report back to the B-Team. All of the reports were encrypted by the commo guys. We wouldn't want the enemy to find out we were ordering a manual for an M-48 Tank.

In just over a week, we received a brand new water cooler.

Top said to me, "*Bac Si*, did you order this?"

I told him I had not and proceeded to remove the water cooler from the packaging and set it up in the team room. When I was finished I filled it with water and plugged it in. How nice. The Army wanted us to have cold water to drink. I was wondering why we hadn't thought of a water cooler before, when I looked at the instruction manual. It was for an M-48 Water Cooler.

"*Crap!*" I wanted a manual for an M-48 Tank and they sent me a manual for an M-48 Water Cooler complete with the water cooler.

This did not discourage the members of our self-appointed tank team. We were going to fire that son-of-a-bitch come hell or high water so we went with Plan B. We climbed back in it and cranked the barrel and pointed it toward the rubber trees. Then we loaded a shell into the breach and attached a string to the trigger. We snaked the string out through the open top hatch and ran it on the ground to a sandbagged bunker some 25 yards away. The whole camp was abuzz with what we were going to do and wanted to watch. We made sure that everyone was well away from the tank and had taken cover behind sandbags and other fortifications.

Operation leaving camp with M-48 Tank in the background.

There was no count down. The senior weapons man pulled the string taut to engage the trigger and there was a huge "KA-BOOM!!" The big gun fired and blew the hell out of a rubber tree 100 yards away. We checked out the interior of the tank and the gun barrel and there was no damage. The 90mm fired just fine.

But that was the first and last time that we ever fired it. We later realized that the breach of the 90mm gun was only two feet away from the back of the interior of the tank. At the time, we did not know how much recoil there would be, but if someone had been standing there behind it, it could have messed them up really bad.

It was a big gun and looked impressive, but actually had limited usefulness for the defense of the camp.

In other words, the weapons guys gave up on it. It was too difficult to move the barrel of the 90mm gun, to aim it, and to fire it. We had mortars, machine guns, a 105 recoilless rifle, and two South Vietnamese 105 howitzers in camp to defend ourselves with. The tank was not practical. But it damn sure looked good on the berm and probably gave the enemy something else to think about. It's only use after that was during an attack, and the company commander of the KKK would climb on top and fire the 50-caliber machine gun.

––––––––––––

A couple of times during my year at Loc Ninh, someone from headquarters would come out and do a property inspection. The camp CO was responsible for all Army property that we were issued and he had to sign for it. The property inspector determined that we had two three-quarter ton trucks, and according to the records, we were only supposed to have one. If we had known that, we would have hidden one of the trucks in the RFPF compound or driven it to Loc Ninh while the inspector was here. The net result was that the inspector ordered that the extra three-quarter ton truck be taken away. I always wondered what would happen if he ever came back and counted an M-48 tank that was not on official property records.

CHAPTER **26**

SONG BE OFFICERS CLUB

▬▬▬▬▬▬▬▬▬

S ONG BE WAS THE capital of Phuoc Long Province, directly east of Binh Long Province. B-Team 34 was headquartered there. I never was at Song Be nor did I have firsthand knowledge of which American units were based there. I do know that they had an officers' club there, or at least were trying to establish an officers' club there. I'll explain how I know this.

The American 1st Division was camped out at the end of the airstrip at Loc Ninh, having been there for a couple of days. There was not much

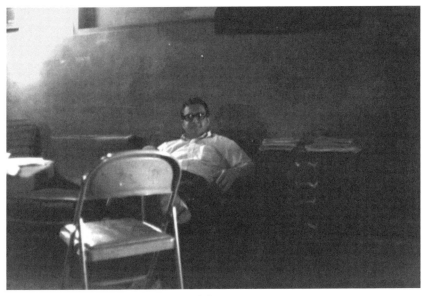

RFPF civilian employee relaxing on one of the Song Be
Officers Club chairs, relocated to Annex 10 Club House.

*Doorway of Loc Ninh Annex
10 Club House.*

going on in our AO at that time. They had had no contact with the enemy at all, the bad guys having chosen to concentrate their efforts someplace else in Vietnam for the moment. Then, a major battle broke out between the NVA and other elements of the 1st Division, further to the south on the way to Saigon. As a result, a call was sent out for the troops dug in at the end of our airstrip to move out ASAP and to reinforce those other units in contact with the NVA.

That day our little airstrip was full of C-130s landing, loading on men and equipment, then taking off to get them to the battle site as fast as possible. Since there were so many planes coming and going, the MPs would not allow us on the airstrip. There must have been 30 or more flights. All available aircraft were being utilized. One of the last of the C-130s to land discarded four CONEX (CONtainer EXpress) containers on the tarmac next to the runway. It then loaded up with troops and took off.

By the middle of the afternoon all of the 1st Division soldiers were gone. The airstrip was quiet again. The four CONEX containers were sitting all by themselves at the side of the runway right where they were dumped. In their haste, the airmen probably had orders to drop whatever they were carrying and pick up and transport the troops to the battlefield further south.

I saw the containers and went to the team sergeant and told him, "Top, there are four CONEX containers that were left out on the tarmac."

"They will probably come back and get them," he said, but I doubted it. A couple of hours passed and I said to Top, "If we leave those containers out there overnight, the Viet's will loot them."

With this he agreed. "Okay, get a deuce and a half and get them into the camp."

I grabbed Goldie (named for his gold front tooth), who was a six-foot tall Cambodian, one of our best mortar men, and a great person to have around. He was the only indigenous person in the camp besides Papa-san, the cook, and his two kitchen helpers, allowed to eat in our compound, though Goldie did not take his meals in the team room with us but in the kitchen with the cook. Goldie and I got a big chain and a deuce and a half and dragged the four CONEX containers into camp. Each one was eight foot by eight foot by eight foot, and very heavy.

Once we had moved them inside, I checked them out. The containers were solid corrugated steel with corrugated steel doors that were padlocked. I didn't think the CIDs were capable of breaking the locks and getting into them during the night, so they were safe for the time being. On each of the doors there was a shipping label with the words "Song Be Officer's Club."

I reported back to Top that the containers were now in the camp and were labeled "Song Be Officer's Club."

I asked, "Can I open them and see what's inside?"

Top was a career soldier. Though I considered myself to be a professional soldier, I did not approach things the way a career soldier did—that is, the Army way or no way.

Goldie, our best Cambodian mortar man.

"No, we have to wait and see if they come back for them," Top said.

Like a little kid I persisted.

"How long do we have to wait?"

"Give it a week," was his answer.

The next day I went off on a five-day patrol, got shot at a couple of times, and when I arrived back to camp on the fifth day, the CONEX containers were right where Goldie and I had left them.

I went back to Top.

"It's been a week, can we open them now?" I asked.

He was okay with it and got someone to do it. Because I was preoccupied with something else, I actually did not see them being opened, but there was furniture, a couple of window air conditioners, two refrigerators, and two deep freezers. The CONEX containers and their contents were then brought into the inner compound so the CIDs would not loot them.

The inner compound was where the A-Team members lived along with the LLDB. It was in the shape of a hexagon and consisted of six main buildings. Each building was three-fourth's underground for protection from mortars. Only the commo and medical bunkers had reinforced roofs to safeguard them from direct mortar hits. There was an additional structure measuring 20 feet by 40 feet parallel with the commo and medical bunker buildings. It had been under construction and was about 90% completed, but was never finished and remained unused.

Lieutenant Sam Stokley, Team XO, at entrance to Annex 10 Club House.

No one knew what to do with the items in the CONEX containers, except for the deep freezers, which we put in the kitchen and the team room where we could use them immediately. I suggested that we finish off the unused building and put everything else in there. Within a week the work on the building was completed and it was ready to be occupied.

We made it our clubhouse.

In the new Loc Ninh clubhouse we mounted the air-conditioning units in a couple of the windows that were above ground, and moved in as much of the furniture from the CONEX containers as would fit. It was great to have an air-conditioned clubhouse that was fully furnished. As you walked into the club on the left was an eight-foot bar with a refrigerator behind it stocked with cold beer and ice cubes for mixed drinks. Just past the bar was a poker table and chairs and beyond that was a seating area with a couple of couches, some stuffed chairs, end tables, and lamps. At the far end of the building was a television set capable of getting one Armed Forces TV station, which was one more than we had before.

We could not fit all of the furniture into the clubhouse, so we gave the rest away to the LLDBs for their quarters. We called our new clubhouse the A-331 Club, ANNEX 10, named after a Special Forces NCO Club at Fort Bragg. I had heard of ANNEX 10 but never been there; all I knew was its reputation as a big hang-out for the career Special Forces NCO's at Bragg.

We would send someone down to Bien Hoa every month to buy beer, Cokes, liquor, and to scrounge for food. A pallet of beer was 88 cases and cost right around 80 dollars. A fifth of booze cost between a dollar and two dollars depending on the brand. The Army would even deliver it to us at our airstrip in a C-130 or Caribou airplane. The way we got money for refreshments was that on the front of the refrigerator behind the bar was a sheet with everyone's name on it. If you had a beer or a drink, you would make a mark next to your name and come pay day, once a month, you had to reimburse the XO for what you had drunk. This system worked out fine. We always had money in the fund to restock the bar.

The clubhouse was a great place to go in the evening to relax and socialize in the air conditioning after being out in the heat and humidity all day. The acquisition of the extra refrigerators and deep freezers also allowed us to keep more food on hand. But it had other benefits as well.

One time a unit was camped down at the end of the airstrip, and we asked their CO if everyone would like a couple of cold beers. Their commander said it was all right, but they could have only two beers apiece and they would pay for them. We stocked the refrigerators and freezers with maybe 25 cases of beer and that evening loaded the cases onto a deuce and a half and delivered them to the American troops.

I don't know if any money changed hands; it wasn't important. I only hoped that this little gesture made those guys' tour in Vietnam a little more bearable.

From that time on, if there was not a lot of nightly contact happening with the enemy, we always tried to provide a couple of cold beers to the US troops camped at the end of our airstrip.

CHAPTER 27

CELEBRITIES

THE SPECIAL FORCES CAMP at Loc Ninh was one of the most active in South Vietnam. We were in almost constant contact with the enemy and were providing a great deal of intelligence on their activities and movement. It wasn't that we were a better team or better individual soldiers than other teams, it was simply because the NVA was making a concentrated effort to gain a foothold in South Vietnam by wiping us out, along with the B-Team located at An Loc. Because of our location we received a lot of their attention.

As a result, not many celebrities ventured out our way, far from the USO shows or the main US bases around Saigon, but a few who wanted to go to where the action was would come to visit us.

Martha Raye had adopted Special Forces almost as her personal family and the men in Special Forces adopted her back as their favorite person in the world. "Maggie," as she was known, was revered by SF personnel. She would not just meet and talk to troops at headquarters, she would fly out to visit and chat with the guys on the A-Teams.

Her first visit to Loc Ninh found me in the field on a five-day operation. Though I did not meet her personally, I did talk to her on the PRC-25 radio. Her call sign was "Mike Romeo" for Martha Raye, and my call sign was "Kilo" for Krizan. The call went something like this:

"Kilo this is Mike Romeo, over."

"Mike Romeo this is Kilo, over."

"Roger, Kilo, this is Mike Romeo, how are you doing?"

We then exchanged pleasantries and talked for another 10 minutes. She seemed very down to earth and not at all like the big Hollywood star that she was. I couldn't believe it—I had watched her in movies! I'm not certain what exactly happened afterwards but she started to feel unwell and was medevac'd out in the middle of the night. When I returned from the patrol my teammates told me how delightful she was.

Troy Donahue, a big Hollywood movie star, also flew in one afternoon on a helicopter with a couple of Special Forces colonels. We all had to line up and as Troy came down the line he shook our hands and made conversation with each of us. The CO took him on a tour of the camp. When they came back from the tour, Troy asked if he could fire one of the captured AK-47's that was sitting out on display.

One of the rumored dirty tricks that some of the top secret Special Forces units did was to plant defective rounds in the NVA ammo depots in Laos and Cambodia. If one of these rounds were fired they caused the weapon to explode in the shooter's face. It was a dirty trick of psychological warfare, meant to cause the NVA to question their own ammo and give our side a slight edge. We were sure that each of the AK-47's and SKS semi-automatic weapons that we had were safe to fire. All of the ammunition that we had captured was checked out by our weapons guys and looked good. Even so, the colonels did not want to take a chance of having a weapon blow up in a big Hollywood star's face.

SSgt Larry Taylor was the light weapons man on the team and they had him take one out and test-fire it before they would let Troy try it. Taylor was not happy about this, figuring it meant that the colonels saw him as expendable. If it blew up in his face it didn't matter; all that mattered was insuring that the big movie star was okay. The AK worked fine and Troy got to fire it, then he and colonels got back on the helicopter and took off. I laughed as Taylor spouted off afterwards in the team room, still pissed.

One time I was in the middle of a five-day, multi-company operation when the Red Cross paid our team a visit. A helicopter flew the Red Cross workers in for an afternoon, during which they served the guys coffee and cookies and chatted with them. The operation that I was on was pretty active, so I did not have an opportunity to talk to them, in fact I wasn't even aware they had been there until I got back to camp. My teammates who did meet them were very appreciative of the fact that they paid us a visit, primarily because there were a couple of real live young American women in the group. I was sorry I wasn't on hand. I hadn't seen a young American woman for quite a few months and would not see one for quite a few more months. The Red Cross visit was definitely a morale booster for the team.

Martha Raye visited our camp again later on in my tour. By now we had our little clubhouse, Annex 10, all nicely furnished and air conditioned. It was stocked with beer in the refrigerator and bottles of liquor behind the bar. This time Martha spent the night in camp. In the evening she sat around with the team in the clubhouse, had some drinks, and played a couple games of poker. Once again I was on an operation in the field and did not get a chance to meet her, though we did talk to each other on the radio again.

"Mike Romeo" and I had become buddies and this time we talked for 10 or 15 minutes. When I got back to camp a couple days later everyone was saying what a great person she was, how she talked and joked and drank with all the guys. She wrote me a note on the message board next to the refrigerator behind the bar that said to call her if I ever got to Los Angeles or Hollywood, and included her phone number. I kept the note and the phone number for a while, but as I did not get to LA until many years later, I never did call her.

Light weapons man SSgt Larry Taylor.

I only got down to the C-Team in Bien Hoa on a couple of occasions during my time in Vietnam. On one of those occasions, toward the end of my tour, I went to the Special Forces club there. It was a huge club with a bandstand where Filipino bands played nightly and the beer was cheap. The bar itself was at least 40 feet long, and up next to the bar I spotted Martha Raye. She was having a drink, surrounded by Special Forces personnel. I thought about going over and introducing myself to my radio friend "Mike Romeo" until I noticed who was in her entourage.

The inner circle close enough to actually talk to her appeared to be made up of colonels and majors. The next group around her looked like some captains and a sergeant-major or two. The third group surrounding Maggie was just standing there while trying to get a look at her. It was full of captains, lieutenants, and high-ranking enlisted personnel. I decided not to crash their little party. Instead, I sat there relaxing and drinking a cold beer. I might have eventually gone over and tried to introduce myself, but after a couple minutes the whole party of Martha Raye and her circle of admirers had moved out the door and were gone.

CHAPTER 28

THREE TIMES

D URING MY TOUR IN Vietnam I was sure I was done for, KIA, three
times. In each instance it was not while engaged with the enemy in
combat—getting shot at, mortared, or ambushed—but three other times
when I knew I had been fatally hit and was dead. It's not like anything else
I can describe. It was an eerie but peaceful feeling that lasted for a second
or less. I truly believed that it was all over. I was dead although my mind
hadn't stopped working and I was convinced that the thoughts I was having would be my last thoughts on this earth.

The first time it happened I was out on a three-day recon mission
southeast of the camp in the jungle beyond the rubber plantation. It wasn't
exactly thick jungle, more like a forest with small to medium-size trees and
tall weeds. We had skirted around Village 2 to avoid being seen or followed.
The second day, as we were making our way through the woods on a road
that could best be described as a goat path, the CIDs could hear someone
behind us. That was what the local VC liked to do—find our patrols and
shadow us to determine where we were going, then try to set up an ambush.
That's why we always took a zigzag route immediately after leaving the
camp. We were easily spotted, and the direction of our movements could
be passed on to the VC.

We were a recon patrol of only about 30 CIDs, so setting up an ambush for the bad guys following us would be difficult. If we had been a
multi-company operation of approximately 150 CIDs, we would stop for
a break and they would also stop. While resting on break we could send
a platoon or two up ahead and have them set up an ambush site. After our
break, the rest of us would pack up and head out. Hopefully the bad guys

would keep following us, and we would lead them right into the ambush as we marched along.

With only 30 CIDs, we did not think we could successfully pull off an ambush with only half, or less than half, of our troops. But we thought of a way to at least shake up the VC a little. We were within range of the two Vietnamese 105's that were in our camp, so we decided that when we stopped we would have them blast the bad guys on our tail with some artillery fire. As we were moving along we radioed back to camp to let them know what we were planning.

To get 105 artillery fire support, we would send one of our teammates over to the big guns and talk directly to them. We did not want any translation errors when we were directing artillery fire. Also, to make things simpler, we would use our maps to give them a grid to fire on. The grid numbers were on our old French maps; we would use an alpha code with letters substituted for the numbers zero through ten, a code that was changed monthly. We would identify not only our location, but where we wanted the first round to be fired. In artillery they might do it differently, but we were not trained in artillery so this method worked very effectively for us. With the first round, you needed to play it safe and call it in a good distance away from you. You would then walk the fire from there by having the artillery crews add or subtract a certain amount of yardage and/or adjust the aim to the left or right.

Once we had stopped, we called in a fire mission giving the coordinates (in code) for the first round. I was sitting on the edge of a B-52 crater with my legs hanging over the sides, anticipating the shelling from the 105's that would be going right over our heads. We called the first round in and then adjusted things from there. After a couple more rounds and further adjustments the last one was exactly where we wanted it—exactly where the bad guys who were following us should have been. We then told the 105's to "fire for effect," meaning to fire 10 rounds and blast the entire area that was being targeted.

I could hear the rounds whizzing overhead and splashing (exploding) right on target, when—WHAM! I was blown into the B-52 crater. I didn't know what had happened. One second I was sitting on the edge of the crater and the next second I was lying on the bottom of it looking up. My only thought was that I had been hit by a 105 round that landed short. I was dead or about to be dead. Why else would I have been blown into the crater with my ears ringing and my whole body feeling numb? I lay there not knowing how much longer I had, until I would lose consciousness or whatever else happened when you died. But then my hearing started to return. I moved my head and saw that my body was intact and that I was not bleeding.

Holy crap, I am still alive.

I crawled on my hands and knees out of the crater to the jungle floor and saw a circular hole in the ground five feet away from where I was sitting that hadn't been there before. It was maybe six inches in diameter with a slight slant, as if it had resulted from something coming from out of the sky in the same direction as the 105's from camp. It was from a "short round"—that is, one that did not go as far as it should have.

Luckily for me it did not detonate, but had just burrowed into the ground. The concussion from the round whizzing through the air and smashing into the ground must have been what knocked me over and into the crater. The entire elapsed time had been a matter of only a few seconds, from the time I got knocked down until I had climbed out of the crater and found the impact hole of the short round.

Once it registered with me what had happened, I screamed at the top of my lungs, "Short round!" and ran as fast as I could away from there. While that sucker was a dud when it hit the ground and created the hole, it could have gone off at any time and taken all of us out. We got going again and began our trek back to camp with no further action. No one on our tail was following us anymore.

Lesson learned. *Never direct fire from the Vietnamese 105's in camp over your head.* They got one short round in on me and would never have that chance again.

————

The second time I thought I was KIA, I was with the team sergeant (Top) and we were setting up a night ambush in the French workers' village a half-mile north and west of the camp. The village appeared to have been built by the French as servants' housing, and was largely abandoned. It was some 20 to 30 structures made of bricks that looked like concrete, with red tile roofs and concrete floors. Most of them consisted of three rooms.

In foreground, the main camp concrete reinforced underground ammo bunker.

One room in the middle was open to the outside with solid walls nearly waist high in the front and back, and an entrance in the front and back. On either side of this middle room there was a door leading to an enclosed room. The outer rooms must have been for sleeping, and the middle room used for cooking. These houses were very different from the ones with thatched walls and roofs and dirt flooring, where the workers on the rubber plantation lived.

As we moved into the village at dusk, Top and I found an abandoned little house and decided to set up headquarters there in the open middle room. The house was right on the main road, which was actually a path that ran through the village. We were setting up an ambush in the village because for the last couple of nights some bad guys, coming from the north and west, had attacked our camp. Intel had it that they were moving through the village on their way to hit us. These were not major attacks, more of a probing and harassment activity. They could have been getting the lay of the land or checking out our defensive positions in preparation for launching a larger attack later, but right now they were mostly a pain in the ass. Intel also indicated that the NVA were building up in our area again, so the 11th Cav had been sent up to Loc Ninh that day to go after some bad guys.

American units that came up to operate in our AO generally bivouacked out at the end of the runway directly east of our camp, and that's where the 11th Cav was that day. They had APC's with 50-caliber machine guns as well as M-60 and M-48 tanks. Compared to our defensive positions in camp, they possessed a whole lot more fire power in their temporary set-up. So that was the situation. The Team was waiting for the enemy to attack; the 11th Cav was dug in behind sandbagged bunkers with barbed wire around their perimeter, ready to respond; and Top and I were preparing to ambush the bad guys if they came through the village.

Things were uneventful and quiet until about midnight. The bad guys must have taken a more westerly route that night. Instead of coming through the village and getting ambushed, they went around us and ran right into the 11th Cav who I'm sure they were not expecting to find at the edge of our camp.

All hell broke out. Machine gun fire, artillery fire, exploding shells. None of it was coming from the enemy but from all of the 11th Cav tanks, APC's, machine guns, and whatever else they were using. The whole night sky to our south was lit up by the firing and the flares.

The problem was that the bad guys, in taking their more westerly route and skirting the village, had ended up getting between us and the 11th Cav. Bullets and tank rounds were now cracking all around us and above our heads. We were taking fire from friendly forces. It wasn't their fault—they were protecting themselves and the camp; we just happened to be down range.

Top was at the half wall on the side from which we were being hit. He got on the radio back to camp, trying to get the gunfire and shelling redirected. He wanted them to let the 11th Cav know where we were and that we were in harm's way. I was hunched over in the middle of the room with my radio operator.

I had just gathered up my pack and grabbed my M-16 and was preparing to crawl over to the wall next to Top, when—BOOM! I was knocked flat on the floor with my face against the concrete. I don't remember actually getting knocked down; all I remember was one moment I was hunched over on all fours and then I was lying face-down on the floor.

I saw dust in the air and felt a pain and heavy pressure in the middle of my back. The thing going through my mind was that we'd gotten hit by a tank round and I had taken it in the middle of my back and I was a goner. It must have been only a second or less that I was lying there wondering if this was what death felt like when Top yelled at me, "*Bac Si*, get over here and quit screwing around!"

I looked up but still felt the heavy weight on my back. I turned over and a whole section of a red roofing tile rolled onto the floor. The round had hit the roof and knocked me down, also causing a roof tile to fall and land in the middle of my back. I scrambled over to Top as fast as I could, then checked myself over. Not a scratch on me, just a slightly deflated ego. It had happened again. For an instant I really believed that I had been killed and was thinking strange thoughts.

At the wall in the house, Top was yelling on the radio to get the tanks to stop firing our way. Finally they did stop, and we then braced ourselves to see if the bad guys would return through the village on their way back to wherever their base was. But all was quiet the rest of the night. They must have again skirted around the west side of the village in their retreat.

———————

The third time I thought that I was killed was much later in my tour, in March or April 1969. I remember it was similar to the other two incidents and it still feels like it happened only yesterday. But I guess that my mind was starting to overflow by that time and I was suffering from combat fatigue. I can't recall a single detail about what or where or how it happened. I only know that it did happen and I believed I was KIA, again.

CHAPTER 29

GOING HOME

THE DAYS WERE DRAWING down. I had them numbered on a calendar on the wall next to my bunk so I could see when my tour in Vietnam would be over. Every 24 hours I would cross another one off. One of the unwritten rules on an A-Team was that during your last 30 days in-country, you should not go on any operations in the field, or they should be very limited. I was told that the first 30 days and the last 30 days in Vietnam were the most dangerous. The first 30, you didn't know what you were doing and were more likely to make a mistake and be wounded or killed.

View of Black Mountains between Cam Ranh Bay and Nha Trang from front window of helicopter ride in May 1969.

The last 30 you thought you were invincible and believed that nothing could hurt you, which made it more likely you'd get messed up.

On an A-Team it really was supposed to be a "team effort." For the first part of my tour, that's the way it was. We all took our turns going out on patrol regardless of rank. But as my one-year tour went on, the CO's on the team rotated out every two to three months, spending the rest of their tours in a staff position at headquarters. Once they had been on an operation and received their CIB (Combat Infantrymen's Badge), they were no longer interested in going out in the field unless it was a high profile mission where there would be a lot of notice from the top.

Besides, they now had extensive MOPSUMS (Monthly Operational Report Summaries) to write up, which also involved the XO and Top and took about a week to complete. My monthly report took about five minutes and was simple: number wounded, number KIA, and a pharmacy requisition. I handed it in after much prodding from the XO and then I was done for another month. Because of the MOPSUM's, the CO, XO, and Top were unavailable for any operations for at least one week a month. Other team members would be on R&R or had gone home, their replacements not yet arrived. It seemed that we were always short of personnel.

With the requirement that we have one company-size operation and one recon platoon operating in the field at all times, the rest of us had to double up on patrols. I would be out on a five-day operation, back for a day or two, out on a three-day operation, back for a day or two, then out for another five days. It just continued on and on. The 30-day rule I now discovered was more bullshit.

Finally, my tour was about to end. I got back from my last patrol with three days left before I had to catch one of the twice-weekly helicopter runs that came on Tuesday and Thursday from the B-Team. A chopper arrived in the morning and a second one in the afternoon of each day. I was going to catch the Thursday morning chopper and get down to An Loc so I could take that same chopper at the end of the day to C-Team headquarters at Bien Hoa, and process out of there.

It was difficult to say goodbye to friends that I had made, though not so much to the American team members. That was because they were like me—one year in Vietnam then home again. The three female nurses, one Vietnamese and two Cambodian, were especially hard to say goodbye to since we had worked together and joked with one another for almost a year. I wasn't much better at saying goodbye to my counterpart LLDB, *Bac Si* Cong, or the interpreters, or some of the CID medics. I tried to keep it quiet that I was leaving soon, but they all knew. They would come up to me and say "*Bac Si* go home America," and it was all I could do to answer, "Yes." I kept thinking of how I was able to leave while they were stuck in the middle of a war with no end in sight. The poor bastards.

But when the Thursday morning chopper came that week I was on it for the start of my journey home.

After the chopper landed at the LZ at An Loc I jumped off with my duffle bag and M-16 and walked the short distance down a narrow road to the B-Team headquarters and reported in. I had to see the B-Team sergeant-major and sign out of the unit. When I was called in to see him, he told me that there was a problem. The helicopter going back to the C-Team headquarters that afternoon was totally full and I would not be able to get on it. That meant that I would have to stay at An Loc through the weekend and wait for the next chopper on Tuesday. That also meant that I would have to be in-country for an additional week.

This was total bullshit.

I explained to the sergeant-major, "I have to get on that helicopter to get to Bien Hoa so that I can get to the Special Forces headquarters at Nha Trang so I can leave the country on time."

He said, "Well you are not getting on, it's full."

"Oh yes I am getting on that helicopter, with all due respect sergeant-major."

"Oh no you're not! It's full of Vietnamese contractors that have to return to Bien Hoa tonight."

I once again respectfully made my case and told him that I had to be on that helicopter. At that point he dismissed me and told me to report back to him at eleven-hundred hour.

I left his office to wander around for the hour or so until 11 o'clock. I didn't get far when I ran into a couple of CIDs from one of our recon platoons at Loc Ninh. I learned that while I was out on my last patrol their entire platoon had been temporarily reassigned to the B-Team and brought down to An Loc. I had not even noticed they were gone, as I was so fixated on going home.

We started to chat some more, me in broken Vietnamese and the two of them in broken English. I don't know which was worse, my Vietnamese or their English. I found out that they were down here for two weeks to dig drainage ditches for a steam bath that the B-Team was having built by Vietnamese contractors. "Steam bath" is actually a misnomer. These so-called steam baths would have a sauna, but afterwards you could get a massage and a blowjob by a Vietnamese prostitute. We called them "steam and creams."

Now I was starting to get really pissed. Not only were they using one of A-331's best recon platoons to dig ditches for their "steam and cream," but they were not going to let me get on the helicopter to Bin Hoa because some Vietnamese contractors needed to get back.

"F*** them."

I reported back to the sergeant-major a little before eleven hundred hour and we went through the same thing—he telling me I'm not getting on the helicopter and me telling him that I was getting on. He went to the next office and spoke to the colonel. Then he came back and said that the colonel wanted to talk to me. He ordered me to stand at parade rest outside the colonel's office until I was called in. I remained standing at parade rest for over 30 minutes.

Maybe they thought that they could wear me down but they were

Fifth Special Forces headquarters in Nha Trang, May 1969.

wrong. I had just spent nearly a year on an A-Team in Vietnam and had been shot at more times than I could count and witnessed horrors that would make normal people ill. Nothing they could do to me was worse than that. It didn't matter to me if they told me to stand on my head. I would do it.

Finally the colonel called me into his office. I marched in and stood at attention then saluted him with one of my best salutes. He returned my salute and said, "At ease."

I stood there at parade rest, not at ease at all, and listened to him tell me that I would not be able to get on the helicopter to go back to Bien Hoa this afternoon as it was full to capacity. I briefly and respectfully explained to him that I needed to get on that flight in order to process out of country and go home on time.

He began to yell at me.

"I said sergeant that you are NOT getting on MY helicopter!" and he dismissed me.

I saluted, did an about face, and marched out of his office. I was immediately confronted in the hallway by the sergeant-major to whom I muttered, "I'll shoot the first Mother F***ing Vietnamese that gets on that chopper before me."

I had some time to kill before the helicopter would arrive and went

Barracks at Nha Trang, May 1969.

looking for the B-Team's little bar. After I found it, I went in, took a seat, and ordered a beer. As I was drinking my beer, a few of my recon CIDs stood in the door and stuck their noses in. I offered to buy them all a drink but they said they were not allowed in. The bar was for "GIs only."

They asked me what was wrong and I said that I was being told I would not be able to get on the helicopter that afternoon, so I would miss going home. I don't remember exactly what their reaction was but they did not think this was right. I drank another beer then went outside and talked to them some more and we all joked around. It was getting later in the afternoon now, almost 3 o'clock, and I knew it was time to go on down to the chopper pad. I was not sure what time the helicopter would be here, probably around 3:30 or 4, but I wanted to be ready to get on it.

I put my duffle bag over my shoulder and kept my M-16 in hand as I walked the 50 yards across the compound and another 30 yards down a rutted two-track road surrounded by barbed wire on either side. The road led to the chopper pad, which was approximately 50 yards in diameter. It was completely enclosed by barbed wire except at the point where the road entered the LZ. There was only one way in or out. When I got there I sat down on a log to wait. While I was waiting, there came a jeep roaring down the road to the chopper pad and in it was the sergeant-major.

"What the hell do you think you are doing?" he yelled at me.

"Going home!" I responded.

He got all pissy and turned the jeep around and roared back to the compound. As I remained sitting on the log waiting for the chopper, I didn't wonder or even care about what they were going to do to me.

I DIDN'T CARE! I was going home.

Shortly before the chopper arrived, 20 of the recon platoon CIDs from Loc Ninh came down to the LZ and stood in a semicircle on the other side of the chopper pad. They all had their packs on and were carrying their M-16's, which didn't strike me as being odd because for almost the entire last year everywhere I went everybody carried a gun all the time. I figured they were there to see me off.

The helicopter circled and landed. A jeep driven by an enlisted man that I did not recognize came down the road and pulled onto the chopper pad. The driver got out of the jeep and threw a mailbag on the helicopter. I walked over and climbed aboard and buckled in. The jeep raced back down the road. We sat there for a minute or two then took off and were flying to Bien Hoa. I was the only passenger. I didn't know what happened to the Vietnamese contractors nor did I care. All I knew is that I was out of there. I was going home.

I also don't know what would have happened if any of the Vietnamese contractors had tried to get on that chopper before me. It would not have been pretty because I would have threatened them with my weapon, if not shot them.

Though I didn't pay much attention to it at the time, I later realized that the CIDs were not just there to see me off. They were locked and loaded and ready to fire if that's what it took to get me on that helicopter. They had my back and their presence at the LZ with their weapons must have been very threatening to the B-Team bigwigs and the Vietnamese contractors. Not that I cared what the recon CIDs would have done. Going home was the best possible outcome, because if there had been a confrontation I was not prepared to live as an outlaw in Vietnam. They would not have taken me alive.

The helicopter brought me to the C-Team headquarters at Bien Hoa, but the memory of the rest of my processing out is blurry. As SF personnel always carried travel papers that said, "Top Secret Courier," I was able to get a flight to Cam Ranh Bay that same evening. But after I arrived I learned there were no more flights to Special Forces headquarters at Nha Trang that day. I ended up at a regular Army barracks prepared to spend the night at Cam Ranh Bay, the last place I wanted to be.

As I was pondering what to do I ran into Tom Roe, my classmate from medics training at Fort Bragg and the guy I had come over to Vietnam with on the same plane. We had both been on the night ambush training mission that had turned deadly, and were even together when we received our A-Team assignments. I told Tom that there were no more flights to Nha Trang and I was stuck here for the night.

"Grab your shit," he said. "I know how to get us out of here."

We walked outside of the barracks and spotted a large helicopter pad capable of accommodating five or six aircraft on a hilltop a half-mile away. We hiked on over there and then stood on the pad with our thumbs out, pointing in the direction of Nha Trang. We were hitchhiking to Nha Trang, north over the black mountains, about 10 miles distant. We kept standing

Medic classmate Sgt. Tom Roe in helicopter during ride to Nha Trang, May 1969.

there with our thumbs out while the helicopters flew over us without stopping, until finally one landed.

We ran up to it and the captain shouted, "Where y'all going?"

"Nha Trang!" we shouted back.

"Climb aboard," he said and so we did.

It was a beautiful flight of only 15 minutes, over mountains that Tom said were infested with VC. And then presto—we landed at Nha Trang. We thanked the captain and the crew, hopped off, saluted them, and walked over to the Special Forces headquarters.

It only took a couple of days or so to process out of Nha Trang before we were on a flight to Tan Son Nhut Airbase outside of Saigon. The plane that would take us home was parked on the tarmac waiting. As Tom and I walked up the stairs to get on board we saw standing at the door "Twiggy"—the same stewardess that had said goodbye to us with a tear in her eye a year earlier.

We told her, "Well we said that we would see you in a year and here we are!"

We sat in the same two seats in the front row across from the stewardess's jump seats and talked to her the whole time on the flight to Hawaii. Fate!

Sitting next to us in the third seat in the front row was an Army medical doctor, a captain. He had been drafted into the Army and spent a year in Vietnam in a field hospital. Once he found out that I was a medic we started to talk about our experiences while in Vietnam, and I told him of the typhoid epidemic I had dealt with. We discussed the various signs and symptoms that the patients had showed.

The captain said, "I've never even seen a typhoid case and hope that I never will."

I agreed with him and said, "I never want to see another one again either, sir."

We landed in Hawaii for refueling and a crew change and said goodbye once again to Twiggy. Then it was off to Fort Lewis, where we were processed out of the Army in 24 hours. Tom and I got to the airport in Seattle on Sunday night with all of our processing-out pay in our pocket, and were trying to get stand-by flights home.

Welcome back to the USA. We both wanted a drink but you could not get anything, not even a beer, in the Seattle airport on a Sunday night. I finally caught a flight to Detroit in the middle of the night and said goodbye to Tom, who was heading home to Kentucky.

I don't know for sure if my little incident with the B-Team in An Loc had anything to do with any medals that I was told I could expect. I was awarded a Purple Heart for being wounded in February. A year after I returned to the States and was back in college, I received in the mail the Bronze Star with a V for actions during the August 1968 battle at Loc Ninh, with the wrong year inscribed.

But I was not awarded a good conduct medal for my service in Vietnam. Normally, officers serving on an A-Team would receive a Silver Star and enlisted men a Bronze Star for their service. Me—nada. But I did the job that I was trained to do and did it professionally. I did the best I could and survived.

EPILOGUE

AFTER VIETNAM

I WAS BACK HOME IN the States. Vietnam was something that I put into my past and I moved on. My new life did not include it.

The third day I was home I bought a new car—a 1969 Oldsmobile Cutlass 442, with four on the floor and 400 horsepower. I was ready to get on with things. I signed up with the Veterans Administration for the GI Bill and enrolled at Western Michigan University in Kalamazoo, Michigan for the fall semester of 1969. After working a couple of manual labor jobs during the summer, I started classes at WMU in September 1969.

College campuses at that time, like the rest of the nation, were full of anti-Vietnam sentiment. There were marches and rallies against the war. I attended classes but did not let on to anyone that I was a veteran, or related any of my experiences there. I wanted to put Vietnam not only in my past but also out of my head. A couple of my best friends at Western knew that I had served but it was not something that we talked about and it was rarely mentioned.

The GI Bill was helpful, covering tuition and books, but did not fully fund room and board and living expenses. Each month I was forced to dip into the money I had saved while I was in Vietnam to pay my monthly bills. I graduated from Western in December 1970 and received a BBA (Bachelor of Business Administration) with a major in Accounting. By now my savings were totally depleted. All I had was my car, my clothes, whatever other possessions that would fit in the trunk of the car, a Gulf credit card that I owed $200.00 on, and a college degree in Accounting.

I got a job as an accountant in a manufacturing business in the Detroit area, and after going as far as I could in that company, took an accounting position in the Kalamazoo area. My accounting degree has been very good to me. It allowed me to work my way up within several industries and hold positions with titles ranging from Accounting Officer at a bank to Assistant Controller, Controller, and Vice President of Finance at various manufacturing companies in and around Kalamazoo. Throughout my accounting career, my Vietnam experiences were a non-issue. They were not something I ever discussed or mentioned to my friends or co-workers.

The only person who has really heard about my experiences is my wife Sue. After a couple of drinks in the evening I would start to tell her my "war stories." She was, and still is, a very patient and sympathetic listener, as sometimes I would get very emotional and repeat the same stories that I had already told her. They are very fresh in my mind and sometimes it seems like they happened only yesterday.

I did join the Disabled American Veterans organization when I returned home from Vietnam, but have never attended any meetings. I wanted to show my support for those who were not as fortunate as me, to survive Vietnam all in one piece. At the time, most veterans' organizations were comprised of guys from World War II or Korea and they held similar views as the general American public at that time. They thought that veterans of Vietnam were suckers and stupid for fighting over there—that we did not fight in a real war. None of us got any respect for how hard we fought and how much we had sacrificed both mentally and physically. When the old guys had returned home from their wars they were welcomed as heroes and received victory parades. When we Vietnam veterans returned home we were despised, ridiculed, and treated like shit.

I did not have any contact with any of my teammates from Vietnam or with my Special Forces medical training classmates until the year 2000. No disrespect to any of them, but I had moved on with my new life and was trying to put Vietnam behind me. I remembered what states some of the guys were from originally, but not having any phone numbers, there was no means of getting in touch with them. Not until the Internet was it possible for us to begin to get connected with each other.

After 30 years I was able to get in contact via e-mail with Tom Reisinger who was the junior medic at Loc Ninh, and Geoffrey Carlson and Pat Loughney who also served with me at Camp A-331. Then popping up on the Internet were some of my medic classmates, Mike Erkel, Bryon

Loucks, and my good buddy Joe Parnar. Via the internet the network of old medic classmates expanded. As we were in contact with each other some of us thought it would be a good idea to have a reunion.

The 50th Anniversary of Special Forces was to be held outside Fort Bragg in Fayetteville, North Carolina, in June of 2002, and we decided to get together at that time. Bryon and Mike took charge and organized a separate reunion for the medics in Fayetteville to coincide with the Special Forces anniversary. Thirteen of us were able to attend along with some of our wives and children. It was good to see my old Special Forces medical training classmates and to learn what they had done after the war. Everyone had moved on and had diverse careers, such as physician's assistants, a pharmacist, a doctor, a fire chief, a forest ranger, teachers, and myself, an accountant.

While wandering around the SF convention floor I ran into Doc', who was the senior medic when I first arrived at Loc Ninh. He was now retired from the military and was attending the 50th Anniversary with his wife. Doc' and I and our wives hugged each other and we talked about our lives and our children. As I was saying goodbye to Doc', he related a story to me. He said that when he was leaving Loc Ninh to go home, the senior medic who he had been filling in for was not scheduled to return for another couple of weeks. Because this meant I'd be on my own for that period, the CO had come up to him and asked, "Doc', how's the new medic (meaning me) doing?"

Doc' said he replied to the CO, "*Dai uy* (Captain), he's good to go."

This made me very proud, knowing that I had been recognized by Doc', a seasoned and professional Green Beret, as "good to go."

Our medics class reunion was a picnic by a motel pool. We all caught up with each other's lives and what we had done since Special Forces. One of my classmates was telling us that he had prostate cancer from Agent Orange and strongly suggested that each of us get a PSA test to determine if we had prostate cancer. I went for a physical once a year and did not give it much thought. But in 2007 I was diagnosed with prostate cancer and in June 2007 I underwent a radical prostatectomy.

Before then I had no contact with the Veterans Administration's health care system whatsoever. At the urging of a couple of my classmates, I went to the VA Hospital in Battle Creek, Michigan. I learned that not only was

I eligible for free medical benefits for life because I was wounded and had received a Purple Heart, but I was also entitled to compensation for the prostate cancer due to Agent Orange exposure.

Then, once I was in the VA health care system, I was diagnosed with having PTSD (Post Traumatic Stress Disorder) from my experiences in Vietnam. After follow up radiation for the prostate cancer in 2009 I am now cancer free. So almost 40 years after my service during the war, I again had to fight for my life—not because of bullets and mortars being fired at me during combat—but from the long term effects of serving in Vietnam. And once again I survived.

Reunion at Ft Bragg, 2002
Front row L to R: Jerry Krizan, Ron Jungling, Joe Parnar; rear row L to R: George Kennedy, John Bianchini, Mike Erkel, Steve Klompus, Fred Holdsworth, John Landry, Julian Aguilar, Tom Roe, Bob Armstrong, Bryon Loucks.

I do consider myself very fortunate. In Vietnam I lost two of my team members on Special Forces A-Team A-331 at Loc Ninh: Lieutenant Joseph J. Miller, KIA July 24, 1968, and Lieutenant John M. Bath, KIA September 20, 1968. Also lost in combat was my friend and SF medical training classmate SGT Benito (Ben) Contreras Jr., KIA September 1, 1968 at A-Team A-323 Trai Bi. Years later, I learned that my good friend, teammate, and partner on many operations and contacts with the enemy, SFC Andee C. Chapman, was KIA on a return tour to Vietnam on June 5, 1972.

As far as the troops (CIDs) that I served with at Loc Ninh, I am sure that many were killed when Loc Ninh was overrun by the NVA in April 1972 after the US had pulled most of its people out of Vietnam. And most of those who did survive were likely put into re-education camps after the fall of Saigon. I assume that the KKK Company, with so many who were sympathetic to the VC, slipped out and returned to being border bandits. I was told many years later by Tom Reisinger that all but three individuals from the two companies of Komerceri Cambodians at Loc Ninh, including Goldie, our mortar man, and Co Banh, our head nurse, were killed in Phnom Penh, Cambodia in 1975.

I am proud and honored to have served my country and I still consider myself to be a professional soldier, even though I did not choose to stay in the Army for a career. I did not foresee a positive long-term outcome for myself by doing so. I am also very proud and honored to have served with the best and most highly trained professional soldiers ever in the world.

APPENDIX A
CODA: THE BATTLE OF LOC NINH, APRIL 1972

W ITH THE REDUCTION OF US combat activities and the subsequent draw-down of US troops in South Vietnam during the period of "Vietnamization," the use of Special Forces A-Team members, assigned as advisors to battalion-sized strike forces deployed to remote camps in the nation's hinterlands, began to be phased out. The Civilian Irregular Defense Group (CIDG) program ended on 12/31/1971, while the *Luc-luong Dac-Biêt* (LLDB—Vietnamese Special Forces), was disbanded the following day. Starting in May of 1970 and continuing to the end of the year, some 14,000 CIDG/LLDB personnel were rotated into the Army of the Republic of Vietnam (ARVN) and assigned to ranger units whose primary mission was to patrol the country's border regions. This could involve reconnaissance missions, engagement with infiltrating enemy forces, and limited cross-border operations.

Non-LLDB CIDG troops were assigned to the Regional Forces—the militia-like district security elements that had come to play a significant role in the pacification of South Vietnamese towns, villages, and the countryside, with the introduction of the "One-War" concept by General Creighton Abrams. General Abrams, who succeeded General William Westmoreland as commander of US forces in Vietnam, had been given the task of implementing "Vietnamization" by President Richard Nixon, which involved enhanced recruitment, training and equipping of the South Vietnamese armed forces, while at the same time achieving a greater level of security for the country's civilian population.

Special Forces Camp A-331 at Loc Ninh, in Binh Long Province, was officially turned over to the 74th ARVN Border Ranger Battalion on September 30, 1970. Binh Long Province was one of 11 provinces comprising MR (Military Region) III, which separated the Central Highlands (MR II) from the Mekong Delta (MR IV) and included Saigon, the capital of South Vietnam. MR III had seen heavy fighting during the earlier years of American involvement in Vietnam. Within its parameters were such contested areas as the Iron Triangle, the Ho Bo Woods, War Zone C, and War Zone D. The senior ARVN headquarters in MR III was III Corps, located in Bien Hoa, an important regional city northeast of Saigon and the site of a large military air base from which both the US and Vietnamese air forces operated.

The dusty district capital town of Loc Ninh had approximately 4,000 inhabitants, most of whom worked on the nearby rubber plantations. By 1972, what formerly was the site of Special Forces Camp A-331, had been converted into a compound that housed the headquarters for the 9th Regiment of the 5th Division of ARVN's III Corps. The A-Team camp at Loc Ninh had seen major attacks by Viet Cong forces in October–November of 1967 and again in August of 1968, both of which were successfully repulsed. On April 4, 1972, Loc Ninh—the village and the regimental compound—again came under attack, this time by main-force NVA troops supported by tanks and artillery as part of the *Nguyen Hue* Offensive, as it was called by the North Vietnamese.

The offensive was conceived by General Nguyen Vo Giap, commander of the North Vietnamese Army, and code-named after Nguyen Hue, the birth name of Emperor Quang Trung, a famous figure in Vietnamese history and national hero, who in 1789 marched his troops north through the jungles and mountains of central Vietnam to administer defeat to the invading Chinese army near the outskirts of Hanoi. *Nguyen Hue* was a daring but dicey plan to deal a knockout blow to the ARVN and force South Vietnam to surrender. No longer would the NVA be pursuing "protracted warfare," which primarily emphasized guerrilla tactics and the harassment of American and South Vietnamese forces while avoiding direct contact on the battlefield. General Giap delivered a speech to the North Vietnamese Politburo in which he declared, "We must fight with determination to win in order to ensure victory, which is near . . . a costly battle is ahead [with] much sacrifice and heartache. . . . Victory is in sight!" he boldly proclaimed.

The *Nguyen Hue* Offensive called for "strong, determined attacks to be launched against the ARVN main force units, inflicting heavy losses." It was characterized by a "three-pronged" strategy that involved striking on three fronts simultaneously. The northern prong would entail NVA main force divisions crossing the DMZ into Quang Tri Province in Military Region I, formerly known as I Corps, with infantry, armor, and artillery as well as a separate drive toward the ancient capital city of Hue, in an attempt to occupy the two northernmost provinces of South Vietnam. As these were the initial events of the campaign that got underway on March 30, 1972—Good Friday on the Christian calendar—*Nguyen Hue* was referred to as the "Easter Offensive" by the Americans and the South Vietnamese.

The second prong of the plan was to include assaults launched from Laos against the cities of Kontum and Pleiku, located in Military Region II, with a drive east toward the coastal province of Binh Dinh. If successful, this operation would essentially cut the country in half along Route 19, which led west from the coast to the Central Highlands.

The third prong of Giap's strategy was to be carried out in Military Region III. While some sort of major attack was not unexpected in this area, because of numerous intelligence reports in previous weeks indicating increased activity and build-ups by NVA forces, the exact location and scale of the impending campaign was not foreseen.

Though Loc Ninh was situated in a vulnerable position near the Cambodian border and to the east of the Fish Hook region (a long-time Communist safe haven and staging area at the southern end of the Ho Chi Minh Trail), the ARVN generals and their American advisors at III Corps and at 5th Division headquarters did not believe that the NVA had the small town in its sights. They remained convinced that the coming enemy assault was most likely going to take place in Tay Ninh, the next province to the west of Binh Long. Initially that appeared to be the case, following a pair of diversionary attacks on outposts north of Tay Ninh City on April 2 and 3, but events commencing on the morning of April 5 would prove them wrong.

The strategic battle plan in MR III, as conceived by General Giap, was for the 5th Viet Cong Division to first attack Loc Ninh, the headquarters of the northernmost district of Binh Long province. The VC's 9th Division was to then launch an assault on An Loc, the capital of Binh Long Province, lying 13 miles to the south of Loc Ninh on Highway 13. (Though these units were designated as VC they were in reality comprised almost entirely of main force North Vietnamese Army troops). Simultaneous with the assault on An Loc, the NVA's 7th Division was to set up in a blocking position south of An Loc on Highway 13 to prevent ARVN reinforcements from advancing north and joining the fight. Once Loc Ninh was overrun and the provincial capital had been captured, An Loc was to be declared the site of the Provisional Revolutionary Government, essentially the capital of all Communist-held territory in the South.

If Giap's strategy succeeded in Binh Long Province, then Saigon—a straight shot of only 65 miles down Highway 13—could conceivably be vulnerable to a *blitzkrieg* attack that would force the South Vietnamese government to surrender. This would not only mean victory for the North but would humiliate the United States and President Nixon, perhaps even causing him to lose the presidential election later in the year. For this purpose, an NVA army corps supported by an artillery division and two armored regiments, was positioned on the other side of the Cambodian border to await the opportunity to move swiftly south on Highway 13 toward the South Vietnamese capital. Ideally, Saigon would be in the hands of the Communist forces by May 19, Ho Chi Minh's birthday, which would be a stunning occurrence and major propaganda victory.

And even in the event that the fall of Saigon did not happen immediately, a secondary goal of the *Nguyen Hue* campaign was to seize and occupy a significant portion of South Vietnamese territory, which would in turn strengthen Hanoi's hand at the Paris peace talks.

Although the town of Loc Ninh had been previously subjected to artillery, mortar, and rocket attacks and seen the human wave ground assaults on the Special Forces Camp in 1967 and 1968, the size and scale of the 1972 offensive was unprecedented. It was the first time that Russian T-54 tanks were used in support of the North Vietnamese artillery and ground attacks in Military Region III. After three days of fierce fighting that saw US air assets, including Cobra attack helicopters, AC-130 Spectre Gunships, USAF A-37 "Dragonflies," and even B-52 Stratofortress bombers coming to the aid of the beleaguered ARVN troops, the regimental compound was overrun on April 7 after most of its defenders had been killed, had surrendered, or had fled.

Seven American "advisors" were caught up in the fighting at Loc Ninh—five of whom were attached to the 9th Regiment, and two who were embedded with the Regional Forces that had a separate compound a short distance to the north of the 9th's. Also trapped in the battle was a French photojournalist for UPI who had come to Loc Ninh at the invitation of one of the American advisors, hoping to experience the war up-close and first-hand. He had wanted to take photographs of NVA tanks, which Intelligence had reported operating in the area.

Of the eight westerners on the ground during the Battle of Loc Ninh, two died, one successfully escaped, and the remaining five, including the French photojournalist, were captured and held at a North Vietnamese prisoner of war camp near Kratie, Cambodia. The Frenchman, who was kept separate from the Americans, was subsequently released on Bastille Day in July 1972, ninety-seven days after his capture. Meanwhile, the Americans would remain as POW's until February 12, 1973, at which time they regained their freedom under the terms of the Paris Peace Accords.

ANNEX J REGRADED UNCLASSIFIED BY
AN LOC AUTHORITY OF DOD DIR. 5200. 1 R
BY _____ ON _____

(C) The NGUYEN HUE Offensive of 1972 began on 30 March with the invasion of northern Military Region 1, Republic of Vietnam. Within a week, the component of the offensive in Military Region 3, which included Saigon, began to unfold. The enemy campaign caught the friendly forces in the area by surprise. Intelligence reports during March indicated that there was little likelihood of an enemy offensive on the scale of that in Military Region 1. While there was the possibility of increased activity near Tay Ninh City, the reports placed great reliance in the ability of allied cross-border operations in Cambodia to keep the enemy divisions busy defending their lines of communication. Critically, there was a lack of mention about the presence of enemy armored forces in the area of Military Region 3. There was no indication that an attack might be mounted on the towns along Route 13, the main route of approach to Saigon from the north. The overall evaluation of the situation was that enemy forces in the Republic retained the ability to conduct battalion size attacks and guerilla, terrorist, propaganda, and sapper activities. Although multibattalion attacks were considered to be possible in the B-3 Front (Kontum, Pleiku, and Darlac Provinces), they were not expected in Military Region 3. This misreading of enemy capabilities as well as intentions seriously affected the level of readiness of friendly forces in the Region (Fig. J-1).

(C) Not until the offensive had been blunted in Military Region 3 were intelligence agencies able to determine what had happened. During the allied operations in Cambodia around the Chup-Dambe areas in November and December 1971, the 5th VC Division had been located between Krek and Snoul. The mission of this enemy force was to prevent the 5th ARVN Division from moving into this area and to resist other ARVN elements attempting to sweep east of the Dambe area. In late December the 5th VC Division had established its base area near Snoul, Cambodia, which is the first significant Cambodian town along Route 13 as it crosses the border. From January through March 1972 this division was refitted and retrained.

(C) In February and March 1972 the 7th NVA Division and the 9th VC Division were refitting and retraining in the Cambodian areas of Dambe and Chup respectively. In late March, documents captured in Tay Ninh Province revealed that ele-

ments of the 9th VC Division were planning to move to Base Area 708 in the vicinity of the Fishhook on or about 24 March. Part of the division was to assemble in a staging area in the southwest portion of the base area. To the east of that location in western Binh Long Province elements of the 272d VC Regiment would assemble where part of the 95C NVA Regiment had already moved. Another unidentified unit was in position north of Camp Tonle Cham and Route 246. The captured documents also indicated that coordination between the 7th NVA Division and the 9th VC Division was possible and that all elements of the 9th VC Division had been trained in urban warfare. The three battalions of the 272d VC Regiment were listed as having received additional training against selected targets.[1]

(C) The objectives of the North Vietnamese and Viet Cong NGUYEN HUE Offensive were to destroy ARVN forces through military victories, to disrupt the Vietnamization and pacification programs, thus "liberating" the countryside, and finally, to take over the government of South Vietnam. To accomplish these objectives in Military Region 3 the enemy developed a complicated tactical plan. The 24th and 271st Independent NVA Regiments were ordered to conduct diversionary attacks against elements of the 25th ARVN Division in northern Tay Ninh Province. This diversion masked the movement of the 7th NVA and 9th VC Divisions through Base Area 708 and into Binh Long Province (Fig. J-2). The 9th VC Division, considered to be the elite division of the enemy force, was assigned the mission to attack and capture An Loc, preferably within five days but not more than ten. A command headquarters for South Vietnam was to be established at the new Communist capital at An Loc on 20 April 1972.

(C) While the 9th VC Division was moving to accomplish this mission, the 7th NVA Division was given the responsibility to block Route 13 between An Loc and Lai Khe to the south and to stop all traffic from reaching or leaving An Loc by road. The 5th VC Division was assigned the mission to move into northern Binh Long Province and attack and capture Loc Ninh. When Loc Ninh had fallen, the 5th VC Division was to coordinate an attack with the 24th and 271st Independent NVA Regiments to isolate the 25th ARVN Division by 1 May. Subsequently, these forces were charged with isolat-

APPENDIX B
BATTLE OF AN LOC, LOC NINH
COMMAND HISTORY, MACV COMMAND GROUP

The following account is a transcription taken from "Command History, MACV Command Group—Annex J, 1972–1973—re: Battle of An Loc, Loc Ninh—Record of MACV Part 1 (10 pages)," a declassified document found in the Vietnam Center and Archive located at Texas Tech University in Lubbock, Texas. A PDF of the complete document is available online by searching the Center's Virtual Vietnam Archive at: http://www.vietnam.ttu.edu/virtualarchive/.

THE *NGUYEN HUE* OFFENSIVE of 1972 began on March 30 with the invasion of northern Military Region 1, Republic of Vietnam. Within a week the component of the offensive in Military Region 3, which included Saigon, began to unfold. The enemy campaign caught the friendly defense in the area by surprise. Intelligence reports during March indicated that there was little likelihood of an enemy offensive on the scale of that in Military Region 1. While there was the possibility of increased activity near Tay Ninh City, the reports placed great reliance in the ability of skilled cross-border operations in Cambodia to keep the enemy divisions busy defending their lines of communication. Critically, there was a lack of mention about the presence of enemy armored forces in the area of Military Region 3. There was no indication that an attack might be mounted on the towns along Route 13, the main route of approach to Saigon from the north. The overall evaluation of the situation was that enemy forces in the Republic retained the ability to conduct battalion-size attacks and guerrilla terrorist propaganda and sapper activities. Although multi-battalion attacks were considered to be possible in the B-3 Front (Kontum, Pleiku, and

Dariac Provinces) they were not expected in Military Region 3. This misreading of enemy capabilities as well as intentions seriously affected the level of readiness of friendly forces in the Region.

Not until the offensive had been blunted in Military Region 3 were intelligence agencies able to determine what had happened. During the allied operations in Cambodia around the Chup-Dambe areas in November and December 1971, the 5th VC Division had been located between Krek and Snoul. The mission of this enemy force was to prevent the 5th ARVN Division from moving into this area and to resist other ARVN elements attempting to sweep east of the Dambe area. In late December, the 5th VC Division had established its base area near Snoul, Cambodia, which is the first significant Cambodian town along Route 13 as it crosses the border. From January through March 1972 this division was refitted and retrained.

In February and March 1972 the 7th NVA Division and the 9th VC Division were refitting and retraining in the Cambodian areas of Dambe and Chup respectively. In late March, documents captured in Tay Ninh Province revealed that the elements of the 9th VC Division were planning to move to Base Area 708 in the vicinity of the Fishhook on or about March 24. Part of the division was to assemble in a staging area in the southwest portion of the base area. To the east of that location in western Binh Long Province elements of the 272nd VC Reigment would assemble where part of the 95C NVA Regiment had already moved. Another unidentified unit was in position north of Camp Tomle Cham and Route 246. The captured documents also indicated that coordination between the 7th NVA Division and the 9th VC Division was possible and that all elements of the 9th VC Division had been trained in urban warfare. The three battalions of the 272nd VC Regiment were listed as having received additional training against selected targets.

The objectives of the North Vietnamese and Viet Cong *Nguyen Hue* Offensive were to destroy ARVN forces through military victories, to disrupt the Vietnamization and pacification programs, thus "liberating" the countryside, and finally, to take over the government of South Vietnam. To accomplish these objects in Military Region 3 the enemy developed a complicated tactical plan. The 24th and 271st Independent NVA Regiments were ordered to conduct diversionary attacks against elements of the 25th ARVN Division in northern Tay Ninh Province. This diversion masked the movement of the 7th NVA and 9th Divisions through Base Area 708 and into Binh Long Province. The 9th VC Division, considered to be the elite division of the enemy force, was assigned the mission to attack and capture An Loc, preferably within five days but not more than ten. A command headquarters for South Vietnam was to be established at the new Communist capital at An Loc on April 20, 1972.

While the 9th VC Division was moving to accomplish this mission, the 7th NVA Division was given the responsibility to block Route 13 between An Loc and Lai Khe to the south and to stop all traffic from reaching or leaving An Loc by road. The 5th Division was assigned the mission to move into northern Binh Long Province and attack and capture Loc Ninh. When Loc Ninh had fallen the 5th Division was to coordinate an attack with the 24th and 271st Independent NVA Regiments to isolate the 25th ARVN Division by May 1. Subsequently, these forces were charged with isolating the remainder of Tay Ninh Province. The general concept for this maneuver was for the 5th VC Division to redeploy from the Loc Ninh area and attack Tri Tam. Simultaneously, the two independent NVA regiments would attack into Hau Nghia and Tay Ninh Provinces from the Parrot's Beak to cut Route 1.

After the common government had been established by mid-May, the 7th NVA Division, 9th VC Division, 69th Artillery Command, 202nd Tank Regiment, and the 203rd Tank Regiment were to attack down Route 13 and the Saigon River Corridor and capture Saigon. Finally, the Thu Bien Subsector and 429th Sapper Group were to attack Bien Hoa. These enemy plans were completely disrupted by the costly attack at Loc Ninh and the failure to capture An Loc, but in the meantime, the enemy set the initial phases of his plan in motion.

The first significant enemy contact in Military Region 3 occurred on the morning of April 2. The enemy attacked the ARVN Fire Support Base Lac Long along Route 20, 35 kilometers northwest of Tay Ninh City, in the Dog's Head area of the Cambodian-Vietnamese border. Formerly called Fire Support Base Pace, the base was overrun within several hours by a regimental size enemy assault. Contributing to the surprise of the defenders was the employment of tanks in support of the enemy attack. Previous intelligence reports had given no warning that the enemy had a tank capability in the area. The fire support base, defended by the 1st Battalion, 49th ARVN Regiment, suffered 10 killed, 44 wounded, and 22 missing, in addition to significant losses in weapons and equipment. Although the enemy force was not identified in the confusion of the battle, it was probably either the 24th or the 271st NVA Independent Regiment.

After the capture of Lac Long the enemy forces continued their move and forced the evacuation of the ARVN fire support base at Thiem Ngon on Route 22 leading into Tay Ninh City from the northeast. The enemy ambushed the withdrawing ARVN elements but did not follow these successes with a thrust against the province capital. The loss of Thien Ngom was more critical that the loss of Lac Long because it guarded the approaches to Tay Ninh City. There was a clear path into the capital had the enemy wished to continue his advance. The failure to press this advantage in Tay Ninh Province was an early indication that this move was a feint, although it was not recognized clearly at the time.

Although the ARVN forces in Military Region 3 had been surprised by the enemy attacks at Lac Long and Thien Ngom, and particularly by the presence of enemy armor, they reacted against what appeared to be a threat against Tay Ninh which was 30 kilometers to the south of the abandoned fire support base. The 25th ARVN Division organized a relief force composed of the 2nd Battalion, 49th Regiment, and the old 32nd, 43rd, and 44th Ranger Battalions. In the confusion of the opening days of the campaign, the mission of this force was not clear. MG James F. Hollingsworth, Commanding General, Third Regional Assistance Command (TRAC), advised General Creighton Abrams, COMUS-MACV, that he did not know whether this force was to link up with the remnants of the ARVN troops that had been driven from Lac Long or to redeploy to the fire base.

In any case, the actions of the 25th ARVN Division relief force were irrelevant to the enemy offensive in Military Region 3. The attack against the fire base was a diversionary attack, intended to draw allied attention from the area of Route 13. There appears to have been little purpose in that operation on the part of the enemy unless that was his goal. There were was no serious attempt on the part of the enemy to continue toward Tay Ninh City, nor was there any effort to maintain continuous occupation of the captured fire support base.

For several days [?] after this initial move against friendly forces in Military Region 3, there was a general lull in the level of enemy activity. However, there were indications of increased enemy activity in the 5th ARVN area of operations, particularly around Loc Ninh and An Loc, the northernmost towns on Route 13. The 5th Division advisors received reports of Viet Cong and North Vietnamese operating in squad, platoon, and company formations during the period April 1–3. TRAC [Third Regional Assistance Command] Headquarters, however continued to place its emphasis on the situation in Tay Ninh Province, in which Fire Support Base Lac Long was located. Attempts to recover the fire base met with some resistance, and a captured North Vietnamese soldier revealed that the main force enemy element in the Tay Ninh areas was the 7th NVA Division.

The enemy operations around Loc Ninh and An Loc in these first days of April were apparently reconnaissance efforts. In addition, some enemy attempts had been made to turn the workers in the *Terres Rouges* Plantation area against the South Vietnamese government representatives in Binh Long Province where both towns were located. On April 4, there began a lull in this type of enemy activity throughout Military Region 3. Probably the enemy was moving into his final positions around Loc Ninh, just before the assault on that district town.

The attack on Loc Ninh was the prelude to the siege of An Loc. What happened at Loc Ninh is difficult to determine; there were few survivors and most of the American advisory detachment was killed or captured. Although the enemy's 7th NVA Divison had been identified coming through Tay Ninh Province, the enemy forces in Binh Long Province remained unidentified for several days after the beginning of the attack on Loc Ninh. Not until the siege of An Loc were friendly forces able to discover the size and unit designation of the hostile force besieging them.

To meet the enemy attack on Loc Ninh, the ARVN Division had the 9th Regiment together with an attached armored cavalry squadron (minus an APC troop) and an attached ranger battalion. At the beginning of the attack, these forces were dispersed. Since there had been no warning that Loc Ninh was an enemy objective, the commander of the 9th Regiment had assigned search missions to the bulk of his force. The attack on the morning of April 5 defeated in detail the forces around Loc Ninh.

The battle of Loc Ninh began in the early morning hours of April 5. At 0400 hours TRAC headquarters received a report from the 5th ARVN

Division that enemy armor had been heard southwest of Loc Ninh moving east toward Route 13. This was the first warning that the 5th ARVN Division faced a force of significant strength and size. At 0650 hours the enemy began shelling the headquarters of the 9th Regiment and the Loc Ninh Subsector Headquarters compound. Soon thereafter, Loc Ninh was subjected to heavy ground attack from the west. Several times the enemy was in the wire before being forced back. The next day MG Hollingsworth reported to GEN Abrams that he estimated the force to have been the size of a reinforced regiment. There were confirmed reports of 60mm and 82mm mortar fires and 107mm rocket fires. There were also reports that 105mm howitzers were being used by the enemy, but these were unconfirmed. Some confusion existed as to whether tanks had been used in the first day's fighting but it appears that at least one tank was knocked out by direct fire from the ARVN artillery with the 9th regiment.

The fighting at Loc Ninh was fierce. American advisors on the ground made extensive use of tactical air strikes. MG Hollingsworth singled out CPT "Zippo" Smith in particular for praise as a result of his effective and brilliant fire direction. In another attempt to break the developing enemy stranglehold, the 1st Cavalry task force with two companies of the 2nd Battalion, 9th Regiment attached was ordered to attack toward the city from its positions north of Loc Ninh. The lead elements of the task force made contact with the encircling enemy just to the north of the beleaguered village. Early in the afternoon, radio contact with the cavalry was lost. It faded from the remainder of the conflict at Loc Ninh, having no influence on the outcome of the battle.

Heavy enemy pressure against Loc Ninh continued through the fifth of April. To the southeast of the town, the enemy had reinforced his attacking elements by noon and launched the major ground attacks. During one of the afternoon assaults, enemy elements attempted a westward crossing of the Loc Ninh runway, which was stopped by well-placed air strikes using CBU's. As the fighting raged, another enemy assault which had succeeded in getting into the wire on the east side of the 9th Regiment's compound post was cut down by helicopter gunships. By nightfall the situation had stabilized, and MG Hollingsworth felt that most of the attacking enemy regiment had been killed.

Early in the morning of April 6, however, the enemy brought up its armor. The defenders of Loc Ninh heard the tanks at the southern end of the runway. Shortly thereafter, an enemy infantry assault succeeded in getting into the wire, and tanks joined the attacks from the northwest and southeast at about 0530 hours. The battle continued for another two hours, seesawing back and forth. MG Hollingsworth observed tanks in groups of seven and eight being beaten back on five occasions. The enemy forces were too strong for the defenders, however, and at 0745 hours the camp was overrun. "Those on the ground at Loc Ninh fought gallantly against insurmountable odds to include 25 to 30 tanks," Hollingsworth later reported to GEN Abrams, "Dauntless and remarkable courage kept them going."

—*MACV Command Group*

IN THE END, GIAP'S grand strategy would prove to be a failure. The *Nguyen Hue* Offensive eventually stalled on all three fronts and the invading NVA forces sustained enormous casualties—100,000 out of 200,000 troops—and lost half of its heavy artillery and tanks. In Binh Long Province the relatively quick victory in Loc Ninh was not followed up at An Loc. The ARVN stood its ground and with the aid of reinforcements and continued massive US air support, the North Vietnamese assault was thwarted. After a ninety-five day siege, ARVN troops succeeded in clearing An Loc of all remaining NVA elements. The *blitzkrieg* on Saigon did not happen and the government did not fall—at least for the time being. (Although time and fortune were not to be on the side of the South Vietnamese.) Loc Ninh, however, remained in enemy hands throughout the rest of the war and did become the seat of the Provisional Revolutionary Government in the South. Loc Ninh also became a major logistical center following the construction in 1972–1973 of a new all-weather road running south from Khe Sanh. It was also the southern terminus of an oil supply pipeline from North Vietnam, as well as a communications hub after the installation of a military telephone system with 12,500 miles of telephone lines. During the 1975 Spring Offensive, one of the major attacks on Saigon was launched from Loc Ninh. The planned blitzkrieg of 1972 had thus only been postponed as the war's final chapter was being written.

— *Robert Dumont*